TONAL MUSIC

TONAL MUSIC

Twelve Analytic Studies

Jeffrey Kresky

Indiana University Press
Bloomington and London

Published in Canada by Fitzhenry & Whiteside Limited, Don Mills, Ontario

Manufactured in the United States of America

Library of Congress Cataloging in Publication Data

Kresky, Jeffrey, 1948–
    Tonal music.
    1. Music—Analytical guides. I. Title.
MT90.K9   780'.15   77-74447
ISBN 0-253-37011-6
1 2 3 4 5 81 80 79 78 77

To my dear friend and
colleague David Olan

CONTENTS

Preface

This book is meant to contrast with the analysis-workbook style of college music class curricula. In place of a multitude of scores accompanied by a meager amount and degree of commentary and "suggestions for analysis," this text offers detailed and thorough investigations, on a variety of levels simultaneously, of individual compositions or fragments. The dual aim here is to provide models for further, independent analytic projects, and to provide a setting for the ongoing observation of theory "in action."

This volume thus fits into the standard college music curriculum in at least two ways. First, the book can serve as the principal focus for a course or seminar in analysis; the number of analyses (one per chapter) is suited to a one-semester span of such a course, and individual student projects can supplement classroom work on the chapter projects. Second, the book can serve as an adjunct text in a first- or second-year theory course, in which case a more relaxed attention to the succession of projects will stretch the applicability of the text to the usual full-year span of such theory courses.

The pieces chosen for study here span the period of common tonal practice, from Bach to Debussy; and so some of the historical development of the tonal system is witnessed. A concluding essay projects this development into the twentieth century, with implications for the analysis of nontonal music. An introductory essay discusses analysis in a general way but, as this book is not intended to teach theory (and thus items from the standard theoretical background are discussed in the abstract only very briefly), it is similarly not intended as philosophy. Much of what is meant herein as "analysis," then, will have to be inferred from the content and spirit of the analyses themselves.

The selected compositions are either readily available to the student in score form or have been reproduced here in their entirety. Thus, accompanying quotations from the score are occasionally scarce. Piano compositions predominate, but in view of the widely representative role of the piano in the tonal era, and in terms of the generally incidental character of the entire timbral domain in most music, this is not a drawback or limitation. In fact, these studies are almost exclusively pitch-rhythm studies, assuming these attributes to be the most fundamental in musical cognition.

In general, matters of notation are treated in a conventional manner, and

should be self-explanatory throughout. Capital letters are used to name individual notes; the name of a triad, key, or scale collection, however, is written
in upper or lowercase letters, depending on the major/minor status of the
item in question.

Finally, it should be noted that no analysis included here pretends to be
complete, not even in the perhaps limited sense in which "analysis" is applied
here. In some cases only certain aspects of the pieces are thoroughly investi-
gated; and in all cases some amount of work is left to the student. The extraor-
dinarily gradual approach taken in the first few chapters, where very little
is taken for granted in a hypothetical listener's encounter with musical matter,
should facilitate the acquisition of student independence at such times.

The studies presented here have grown jointly out of my experiences
as a graduate student at Princeton and as a teacher at William Paterson
College. Though no individuals have borne directly on this work, I would
like to mention those musicians whose ideas about tonal music and musical
coherence in general have deeply affected the course of development of my
own musical thought: Milton Babbitt, Benjamin Boretz, J. K. Randall, and
Peter Westergaard. Mr. Westergaard's *An Introduction to Tonal Theory*
(W. W. Norton) presents a view of the tonal system that has influenced this
work generally, and I recommend that text enthusiastically. For the same
Schenkerian notions in a specifically analytic context I recommend Gerald
Warfield's new book, *Layer Analysis* (David McKay). And readers specially
interested in ideas suggested in my Conclusion I direct to George Perle's
well-known *Serial Composition and Atonality* (University of California).
In conclusion, I take pleasure in crediting David Olan, to whom this book
has been dedicated. He enthusiastically studied and commented on the work
as it developed, and his responsive observations and clarifications have been
appreciatively incorporated.

Introduction

Analysis, of whatever kind, is a quest for understanding. Analysis of musical compositions, then, ought to be a vital and fundamental musical activity. Since few musicians would deny that listening to music is the most basic musical activity, the relation between listening and analysis may help point out the importance of the latter.

When we listen to a piece of music we usually do not hear each pitch as an isolated event; if we did, the succession of such events would mean as little to us as would an English sentence whose words we understood only as individual, unconnected, recognizable elements. Rather, at a great variety of levels (depending, certainly, on the complexity of the piece and the degree of our familiarity with it and with the genre of which it is an instance) we hear an unfolding of relations. By relating details to each other, we can discover meaning in a musical passage: for "meaning" is that which we ascribe to something that does not refer to itself alone.

Analysis consists of expressing, in verbal or other nonmusical communicative form, the relations we perceive when we listen to and appreciate a piece of music. As the verbal counterpart to listening, then, analysis derives from and depends on the listening experience crucially. On the other hand, there is a very interesting and profitable feedback from analysis to listening. For if by generalizing or projecting from our listening experience, or by drawing upon models of relations from theory (which is, after all, a kind of codification of listening experience), we can discover some relation among musical details that we have not previously heard in a piece, then, when we learn to *hear* such a relation, our listening experience may be enriched.

The close relation between listening and analysis is thus a flexible one. And we can regard the relation between theory and analysis as similarly flexible. Analysis would seem to follow theory, in the sense that we analyze according to models contained in theories—the model of the neighbor-note formation, for example. On the other hand, theory might seem to be just a formalization of the kinds of things we find, through analytic experience, to be useful reminders of the shared characteristics of certain kinds of pieces.

At any rate, as will be shown in the first chapter, too heavy a reliance on theoretical (or, as will be seen later on, historical) models may prove detrimental to analytic technique and discovery. And so our first analyses tend to develop models already familiar from theory as they are needed. Hence the preliminary analyses are very painstaking, and may seem tedious or even trivial. The value of the approach, however, will have to be judged as the chapters proceed.

The chapters present a series of analytic studies, one composition per chapter. The approach throughout, but most visibly at the start, is (in keeping with what has just been said in regard to theory) heavily dependent upon discovery on the basis of observation. That is, a piece of music is viewed as a collection of data, and, by clarifying observations on this data, we come to say how we feel about the events we encounter in a piece. It is necessary here to restrict the domain of these feelings to the kind that are readily shared by many listeners, and thus relatively independent of a particular listener's particular emotions. That is, such feelings as patriotism, romance, or fear may play an important part in someone's experience of a piece; but we will safely stay within the range of more communicable and verifiable feelings, such as can be derived from decisions about relative importance, size, appropriateness, and expectation. It is quite easy to see how certain emotions could be generated from such situations: the frustration, for example, at not encountering an appropriately important detail at a time when it is expected.

Perhaps reference to some familiar analytic situations will clarify some aspects of musical analysis. A chemical analysis, for example, is designed to break down a perceived substance into its component structural parts. The behavior "at the surface" of the substance is then understood in terms of that structure. A psychoanalysis, to refer to another familiar example, seeks to explain a person's surface behavior in terms of underlying motivating forces. In both these cases the notion of a *conceived-of* "subsurface" inferred from a *perceived* surface is evident.

Since the structure is very much more general than the surface (which is detailed, and is a particular *expression* of the structure), the notion of *buildup* also seems relevant. A structure is a "background"—a kind of aerial view of a complex and extensive object, like the plot summary of a novel. Analysis often results in a buildup of the surface (in music, the piece itself) from a background, through successively more complicated and detailed levels or stages. Thus the surface data gradually become explainable, accountable, or comprehensible *in terms of* more general, background constructions.

Finally, some comment on the nature of the data we will be observing is in order. Disregarding cultural and historical contexts, we can see pieces most directly as collections of sound events. These events are characterized by the attributes of pitch, rhythm, dynamics, and timbre (with a possible fifth attribute, articulation, consisting, really, of combinations of the other four: staccato, for example, a combination of rhythm and dynamics; accents, a matter of dynamics and perhaps timbre). However much one appreciates the colorful features of dynamic and timbral differentiations, one can, with very little reflection, realize the fundamental positions of pitch and rhythm in this scheme. Our feelings about the identity of the tune "America," for example, derive from our recognition of the invariant pitch-rhythm complex that is always associated with that melody; played loudly, or on a flute, or smoothly, the pitches (and their rhythms, the two attributes being, surprisingly, not entirely separable) seem to carry the essential information. With incidental attention paid to the supporting aspects of non-pitch elements, then, our principal attention will be fixed on the pitch domain, with rhythm playing the major projective role.

The questions we have raised here are without doubt very complicated, and disturbingly elusive. To deal with them more thoroughly and conscientiously would probably mean postponing actual analytic endeavor for a long time. Perhaps a good compromise is simply to begin the studies presented in sequel, in the expectation that the ensuing activity will inspire much personal thought on these matters, and perhaps serve as a stimulus for the development of one's own attitudes.

TONAL MUSIC

Analysis of a
Typical Tonal Progression

To gain experience with simple material, as well as to establish a model for analytic activity, we can begin by studying a typical tonal progression, which, by agreement, we can temporarily regard as a complete composition. (Ex. 1–1).[1] We proceed from the observation that this music is a coherent-seeming succession of sounds, and on the assumption that a good deal of this coherence ought to be expressible verbally. That is, we strive to say just what it is we feel unifies the events of this piece.

Perhaps the first pitfall to avoid would be the temptation to describe the piece simply as "the succession I–IV–I–V–I in C major," a description that may tend to dismiss the piece as already analyzed, and one that, we shall see, may also tend to hide behind a façade of labels our feelings about and responses to the notes and the way they interact. (And only the communication of these feelings can enlighten others about the coherence we experience.) Certainly such labels were invented to mean something significant and useful, but we may all too easily forget or bypass the *depth* of their significance and thus miss much of the coherence these convenient names may actually imply.

---

1. It should be understood that this piece has not been specially constructed to yield any particular amount of impressive commentary, but merely represents a typical-sounding tonal utterance.

Ex. 1-1

A better path, from this point of view, might be to begin responding to the music in as basic and unconditioned a manner as we can imagine. In other words, we try to react to the piece not from the perspective of training or cultural background, but rather as if the sounds in the music were new and alien: as if the sense of these sounds and the story they tell had to be discovered anew, even though the progression is so familiar. The effects such an approach will have on our musical understanding can only be judged when experienced, and so further justification can be delayed. But an analogy to this method may be useful, just to clarify what we are trying to do. Pretend that we are playing this composition to some foreign listener—that is, someone not acquainted with tonal music. Imagine that this hypothetical listener has very acute hearing and a liberal imagination. In order to make sense out of this piece, such a listener would have to discover very basic, seemingly trivial truths about the sounds and their relations. If he claimed that the piece were incoherent, that the choice of events seemed random to him, we could not change his mind very well by saying that the coherence of the piece lay in its describing I–IV–I–V–I of C major. It is hard to see how such an explanation could enlighten him or make him hear what we hear. But if we could explain to him in detail just how we feel about these notes— eventually, perhaps, including the concept (which would then rest on a good deal of prior understanding) of the development of such labels— he could conceivably follow the story of the piece, and ultimately experience the music the way we do. We will, then, pretend to be addressing (or, indeed, pretend actually *to be*) this imaginary listener.[2]

---

2. We should bear in mind that our response to *his* music is likely to resemble his response to ours. So we should not condemn some alien music for being incoherent just because we find nothing to follow in it. Whether or not the music may ultimately appear to possess no discoverable coherence, at best we could initially say only that *we*—and not necessarily the music—are confused. Perhaps, then, he could teach us about the coherence of his music; and then, were we as open-minded as we propose him to be, we might be able to appreciate his music, too. Such a notion can relate as well to foreign-cultured (e.g., Asian) music as to, say, twelve-tone music. The analogy to human language may be instructive here: surely we don't wish to say that Chinese is incoherent just because we are not able to make sense out of Chinese statements.

To follow this kind of path, we must choose some very obvious starting point, an observation resting just on the level at which the piece is no more than an even-valued succession of five equally thick sounds (with the final entry equal to the previous four in duration). If our listener is sensitive to pitch discrimination only to the point of being able to distinguish "same as" and "different from," he can still follow our initial observation: the first and last events, those that are the most striking by virtue of their temporal extremity, are identical in content. Such an observation, trivial as it may seem, nevertheless instantly imposes some rudimentary coherence on our experience of the (hitherto) random-seeming music: the piece appears now as a kind of excursion *from* an identified place and *back to* the same item.

At least one other aspect of the music aligns with (that is, tends to support or suggest) this conclusion. The first and last events, being downbeats, are identically stressed. This observation is a matter of real response on the part of the listener, and depends on his sensitivity to articulative distinctions. That is, this is clearly not just a matter of graphic notation and our understanding of its conventions and indications. Presumably the careful performer will interpret the downbeats in such a way as to make clear the distinction between them and the notes appearing elsewhere within the measure. Our acute listener can then respond to these stresses, and this response, as well as the notion of firstness and lastness, could lead him to the discovery of the two-chord identity.

Finally, matching simple before–after and longer–shorter discriminations with our basic same–different pitch distinctions, we discover that the final arrival (at what is now a kind of "home base") represents a kind of affirmation of the starting point, since the last chord is a good deal longer than any of the others.

At this point our experience is still very rudimentary in the sense that the chords occurring between these two posts, the connecting material, are unclassified; the connecting links do not yet contribute significantly to the picture of the succession. But a breakthrough is just around the corner, as we note that the *middle* chord of the group (which, after all, is stressed as a result of the performance conventions regarding third beats of $\frac{4}{4}$ measures) is yet another duplication of the outer pair. Our picture instantly takes on more decisive shape: the piece now seems to proceed from its first chord to its last (identical, reaffirmed) chord *by way of* this familiar, and therefore appropriate, intermediary station. Ex. 1–2 represents the progress of clarity of this picture as it has unfolded

Ex. 1-2

a) chords   1   2   3   4   5   (at first, as separate, unrelated items)

become viewed as:

b) items   1   2   3   4   1

and then as

c) items   1   2   1   4   1   (by the application of the identity observations)

through these observations. We should point out that at this stage of understanding chords two and four of Ex. 1-2 could just as well be referred to as "x" (= "not chord one"), since so far we have only distinguished between things that are chord one and those that are not.

If all this seems terribly trivial, imagine that these chords were not simple, familiar triads, but complex, unfamiliar sounds, such as may be encountered in some contemporary music. Such analysis, and the minimal understanding it brings, might surely help then, and, for practice, we do not shrink from making it explicit now.

Because of the size of our chord succession, the latest observation will bring additional coherence to our experience of the notes: between the elements identified at this point there are only *single* items now (whereas before, between identified first and last chords, there was a whole uncharted region). So we are in a position to paraphrase the story of our piece as follows: begin somewhere, move away, return momentarily, move away again, and return finally. One chord event performs, alone, one step in this plan. Put another way: we go from first to last chords by way of the middle stop, and from first to middle (and from middle to last) by way of less familiar intermediary stations.

This situation suggests that we next focus on the exact nature of chords two and four, these "non-one" chords, in search of some understanding of how these connecting chords may be appropriate, well-chosen, unifying links, and not just randomly supplied filler. In order to do this, we must digress momentarily to clarify some aspects of our (the hypothetical listener's) hearing.

First we must assume the notion of octave equivalence. Though this is not necessarily a universal way of hearing a series in which each pitch has a frequency twice that of the previous one, the functional equality of such pitches (as indicated by their common letter name) is obviously a very common part of most hearing.

Now once we regard any C, for example, as sounding much the same as any other C in the entire pitch range, then the notion of equivalence of interval-complements follows directly: not only will, say, F up to the next C make a sound that shares much with the sound made by the F up to some higher C, but also the interval between this F and some *lower* C (C's being more or less equal in some sense) will join this equivalence group. To generalize: intervals and their "complements" (what are imprecisely called "inversions" in usual tonal-theory discourse) share certain essential sonic qualities, and, therefore, functions. Fourths resemble fifths, minor seconds resemble major sevenths in some readily apparent surface manner.

Now the implications here are as follows: if we examine the first chord of our piece we find that it contains (only) a minor third, a major third, and a perfect fifth. This is the intervallic information stored in the chord, some of it explicit (the two thirds), and some of it latent (the fifth, which is not directly heard as an adjacency). The characteristic sound of chord one would seem to reflect the component intervals that form the chord. Now if we examine the second chord of the succession, we discover that it introduces no new intervals—none, that is, that are fundamentally different from the point of view just developed. That is, chord two presents the same intervals, or their complements, as found originally in chord one: a major third, a perfect fourth ("=" perfect fifth), and a major sixth ("=" minor third). Since we already know that chord three is a duplication of chord one, we can now see at least one way in which chord two is an appropriate link between them: it is made out of the same essential intervallic materials. And similarly, chord four contains, in rearrangement, just (and only) these same intervallic "classes." So its place as a connector of chords three and five is equally secure. And so we see that the entire string of chords that constitutes our piece makes use of a very limited, unified, interval-type vocabulary, and all the chords represent the same essential combination of interval types (major-third type plus minor-third type plus perfect-fifth type).[3] All these types, of course, are introduced in the first chord, and so the

---

3. Of course this is really what we mean when we say that they are all triads, and it is at this point that we could begin to use the label meaningfully. But prior to the realization that all major and minor triads, in all inversions, possess the same intervallic information, it is obviously better to discover the underlying unity in such a passage, thus gaining the convincing demonstration of some coherence (that can subsequently be assumed when the triad label is being used).

rest of the piece seems to flow naturally (at least in this sense) out of the initial event.

Viewed as a series of vertically significant events, our piece is beginning to show a certain comforting amount of coherence. We now know that to go from chord one to its duplicate, chord three (which in turn will be experienced as the overall link to chord five), we use a familiar (that is, not entirely new or unrelated) means: a chord that just recombines, with different pitches, the same interval types. In fact, the fourth-fifth type, the only latent interval in chord one, becomes explicit (an adjacent interval) in chord two. So the move to chord two is additionally an exploratory and developmental move, exposing as it does a property or characteristic present but not entirely apparent in the first chord.[4] And from the way chord four is arranged we can see how it is a kind of balance or mirror of chord two (whose essential function of linking it shares)—here the fourth is on top.

It may seem at this point that our analysis is complete: we have a way of following the progress of chord one through each of the successive chords, each of which seems to perform a minimal function in the overall progress, and each of which derives its shape and essential sound from the initiating chord, which seems to be the "subject" of the music. But we can apply a useful test here by hastily conjuring up another piece that fits the description thus far of our present composition, but which otherwise differs; the degree of difference within the same general plan, or really the degree of significance of this difference, may suggest how much about the original is yet unanalyzed. That is, some not yet understood aspects of our original, omitted in the construction of our test case, may render the latter less coherent. As far as our analysis goes, we could just as well be describing the piece in Ex. 1-3. Chords one, three, and five are connected by interval complexes that relate to the original and to each other in all the ways so far observed. Yet, by normal tonal

Ex. 1-3

4. An analogy to fiction may be useful here: the unfolding of the life of a character will continually reveal aspects of his or her personality that are presumably present, though not necessarily explicit, at the outset of the book.

standards, this piece doesn't seem to cohere nearly as well as the original: we must have overlooked some fairly basic aspects of our piece, despite the fact that we have been looking at it so closely.[5]

Here we might ask ourselves some question like, "what makes chord two of Ex. 1–3 seem a funny choice to follow chord one (in relation to further, as yet undiscovered appropriateness of chord two in the original)?" One direction to follow may be that of actual pitch content; it should occur to us that in examining our original chords we have looked only at intervals and not at the actual pitches that form these intervals. We could begin by noting that, in the original, chords one and two share a note; this note is displayed prominently on the bottom of chord one, and thus is easy to hear and follow.

This area of investigation is already bearing results, and continues to do so as we check chord four (the other point of difference between Examples 1–1 and 1–3). Here we find another shared pitch between chords, a retention of the (significantly, prominent) top pitch of chord three into chord four (and of course over to chord five). We previously noted, when looking at the intervals, that chord four performs its link function in a way that mirrors the performance of chord two (with the fourth, the newly discovered interval, placed at the opposite end of the chord). Here, with these retentions, we see another way in which the precise form of chord two conditions (is mirrored by, is developed by) the precise form of the later link: bottom-note sharing has become top-note sharing. We can further observe that the two pitches used in this sharing are just the notes that span and outline our original chord, C and G. So, a great deal has been made out of the two notes we are most likely to notice in the first chord of the music.

At the same time, this direction of thought really suggests another, for in isolating these sharing events, we are actually paying attention to an entirely different dimension of the music: the lines. Our previous observations have all been about the vertical aspects of the music, the chords. We immediately see now the wide leaps of Ex. 1–3, as opposed to the close fittings in the horizontal plane of Ex. 1–1, and can proceed to

---

5. Of course, this kind of test could have been applied all along the way, whenever we may have felt that we had discovered sufficient coherence to account for our satisfying experience of the piece. At the outset, for example, consider a piece whose first and last chords are identical, but whose other chords are random poundings of the fist on the keyboard.

investigate the precise nature of the lines of our piece. We may have
no reason to prefer linear steps to large leaps, but at least our Ex. 1–3
calls attention to the linear aspects of the original piece, and, in suggesting what elements of the music to look into for undiscovered coherence,
our test has done what it was designed to do.

So in isolating the detail C–C–C from the bottom of the first half
of the piece we have actually identified a line segment; the complete
line, the succession of bottom notes, reads C–C–C–B–C. In parallel, we
can isolate the top line, which perhaps is the one most often thought of
as a line (in the sense that it is a "tune"; but notice that the pitch sharing
takes place in both areas, and suggests the view of the bottom notes as
a line as well). In any case, attention to both successions is immediately
rewarding, since we can relate the two lines by shape:

top-line shape   *bottom-line shape*

Clearly the two shapes are the backwards mirror-images of each other.
It may seem more difficult (aurally) and less obvious (intuitively) to
isolate into a line the remaining notes (the middle slots of the chords); but
if we do, the results in terms of our quest for some rudimentary linear
coherence are heartening. For this middle-line shape:

appears as a combination of the most interesting features of the two outer-
line shapes. So as we read up or down the piece, thinking of it as a group
of lines sounding together, we see it as a group of related items. This is
particularly satisfying in view of our previous demonstration that, when
pictured from left to right (or right to left), the piece appears as a group
of related *chords*.

Since this observation could be made of any three such related lines,
independent of the actual shape of the "first" (referential) one, the next
step would seem to be to study one of these lines as an independent item,
capable of performing a function *for this piece* (just as we did for, say,
chord two). What can we make of the first-noticed segment of the top
line, G–G–G? Quite simply we can view it as a very basically elaborated

form of just "G." That is, the function of repetition or retention can be to prolong the existence of a note past its original time span. Such a notion may seem unnecessarily simplistic, but it is useful even at this level to regard such activity in terms of more generalized function.

To grasp the meaning of the complete line, then, we need to interpret the "curved" part of it, that which flattens out into G–G–G. For this segment, G–A–G, we need to invoke some notion of embellishment or prolongation just slightly fancier than that of straight rearticulation (repetition). There is certainly nothing imperative about the notion that G–A–G is taken to "mean" G; but perhaps the closeness of A to G, in contrast to the greater distance between adjacent notes *in* the chords, can in this piece itself suggest the idea of the standard tonal "neighbor embellishment."

If we accept or define the neighbor-embellishment shape G–A–G as indicating a prolongation, for the duration of the unit, of the first note of the group, or as a *deviation* from the flatter, less elaborated G–G–G, then, putting together the two segments of the line, the succession seems to reduce, in overall meaning, to the same conceptual "G."

Then, in similar fashion (but again, like the variations witnessed in the chordal domain, not *identical* fashion) the bottom line, consisting as it does of segments centering on the note C, seems to express *its* own first note: C–C–C–B–C (= C–C–C + C–B–C = C + C = C).

Finally, proceeding to the middle line, which we have already related by shape to the outer lines, we can, invoking the same simple notions of shape meanings, understand it as an elaborate expression of *its* first note: E–F–E–D–E = E–F–E + E–D–E (the split here of course is suggested by the identification of each three-note curve with a congruent curve in another line), and E–F–E + E–D–E = E + E = E. E is thus expressed or prolonged by a combination of the more interesting forms of the C and G expressions of the other lines.

The result of these various observations, most of which have depended simply on common perceptual sense and a minimum of labels or predisposed notions, is a fairly tight picture of coherence in the chordal, vertical domain (the succession of chords connecting chord one with its duplicate, by way of various related chords); and a separate view of the piece as a group of similarly related lines, which emanate from their initial notes the way the chords grow out of the first chord. But since the first chord is, naturally, nothing but the simultaneous isolation of the first notes of all the lines, the way to join these two views into a powerful, unified picture is amazingly direct.

We can make explicit this intuitively clear juncture as follows: the top line expresses G, the middle line E, and the bottom line C. So together the three lines prolong, express, or embellish the group C–E–G, the C triad. But precisely this group of pitches served as our basic reference for the reading of the chord succession (the chords told a simple story about the C triad, moving away and returning in the particular way described). So the same item, the C triad, serves simultaneously as reference or index for the linear *and* vertical unfoldings. The result of this sameness of reference or base is a curious kind of matrix, one which is unique to the tonal system as a whole, and remarkable in its flexibility, expandability, and capability of embracing an enormous variety of surface manifestation.[6]

We have gone a long way, and perhaps in a somewhat tedious fashion, toward pointing out the rather surprisingly vast coherence exhibited by such an innocent-seeming, perhaps trivial, but certainly typical tonal utterance. All our observations have served to answer the question, "What makes this group of sounds a piece?" Let us reverse our direction for a moment and ask whether there is some way in which this example of music seems insufficient as a composition. The double bar at the end of Ex. 1–1, an artificial indicator of compositional completion, was, after all, placed there arbitrarily. As listeners, what do we make of this agreement?

For example, we may actually feel it to be a detraction that the first and last events in this piece are *precisely* the same; this detail may seem to rob the piece of a sense of overall accomplishment or direction. As a matter of fact, we *are* accustomed to tonal pieces (generally) beginning and ending with the same chordal complex (the tonic triad of the piece), but usually these chords appear in different forms: most frequently, though both root-position tonic triads, these first and last chords feature

---

6. This unification should go some distance toward countering the objection that, say, A of chord two is claimed to function not only as a member of a chord (the first rearrangement of the chord one intervals, with its linking function to chord three), but also as a neighbor to G (in the other dimension, the top line that flows from the initial G). The point is, A is *both* functions stored in *one* articulator. In this sense tonal music is like a crossword puzzle: single items (notes) function simultaneously in two dimensions, just as the letter "u" can be a part of the word "run" in the horizontal plane of an array of words, while simultaneously, and every bit as meaningfully, be a necessary and functioning part of the word "jump" in the vertical plane.

different top-line notes. Often this difference can prove crucial to a sense of ultimate shape, direction, or accomplishment. And we see that this overall shaping may be discoverable *in the melody line*. (This question of accomplishment may similarly be at issue in the relative placements of the IV and V chords in this little piece, a matter we have avoided in our discussion.)

We do indeed seek directionality in tonal music, a sense definitely lacking in the composition studied in this chapter. While we did witness a certain amount of development (the conditioning or informing of later events by prior ones), the piece viewed as a whole was essentially static. In order to begin seeing a developmental process in action we turn now to a simple melodic slice of a real tonal piece.

Analysis of a Theme
from a Haydn Symphony

In studying a theme from a symphony movement we are, of course, looking at a fragment of a composition, and this retreat from the "complete" composition studied in the previous chapter may seem out of order. But the reasons for such a move lie in the twofold nature of the slicing that produces such a fragment. First, we have isolated a segment of the total span of the piece—that is, we proceed a little way into a composition, and then stop. The reason for this is simply that tonal pieces are generally lengthy, and if we immediately proceeded to study a complete, real composition (as opposed to the construction of chapter 1) we would soon lose our way in its length, and probably be forced to sacrifice some understanding of detail for the sake of some comforting overall view. Second, we have isolated a certain portion of the depth of the piece—we move a little way *down* into the music, and lift out only the melody. The reason for this approach is that we will be looking, chapter by chapter, at tonal pieces, and tonal pieces feature melodies as prime carriers of information. Furthermore, we discovered at the end of the last chapter that the behavior of upper lines can affect compositional directionality. So we need to gain experience with a melody in isolation, and then apply this experience to such lines embedded in thicker textures.

At the same time, such a decision involves certain handicaps. Since this *is* just a portion of a piece, we may not see the completion of structures unfolding in time. And since the music is also just a single layer, we are likely to be presented with incomplete information about the way a note strikes us (we will be able to relate a note to its neighbors to the left and right, but not to those notes sounding with it). We must be aware of the artificiality of these circumstances and accept this drawback for the benefits outlined initially. Our conclusions will have to be temporary, subject to the perhaps great change brought about by what *precedes and follows* the fragment as well as what *harmonizes* it.

The subject (Ex. 2–1) is the theme of the principal opening section of the first movement of Haydn's Symphony #104 ("London"). As we

Ex. 2–1

NB: This last note does not actually appear in the score, but is sounded an octave higher, where it initiates a new phrase. It does not significantly affect our analysis to round off the fragment this way.

proceed with observations and tentative conclusions we will bear in mind very closely the kinds of relations we drew in the previous study, as well as the additional expectation of *directed, motivated* continuity (as suggested at the end of chapter 1).

Obviously the initial observation made on the piece of the first chapter, that of identity, will not serve here, for the first and last notes of the Haydn are not the same. But the notion of identity was used in that discussion for *internal* slicing as well as for overall motion, and in that sense this kind of observation provides an immediate entry into the world of this piece. We need only notice that measure 9 initiates a restatement of the original music. In fact, measures 1–4 are exactly duplicated by measures 9–12. What makes this repetition particularly striking is that it is separated from the previous music by a silence: measure 8 contains the only rest in the theme, and this punctuation, together with the repetition it brings about, prompts us to view the piece in two principal sections: from measure 1 up to the silence, and from the repeat-point up to the end (Ex. 2–2). Even if we had trouble noticing the dupli-

Ex. 2-2

m. 1	m. 16	undifferentiated view
m. 1	m. 9 m. 16	sectioned view composed of two related blocks

cation at first, the uniqueness of the silence might draw our attention to the repetition it punctuates; at any rate, we can proceed to notice that this view splits the music into two equal sections, and we need no longer hear the music as one undifferentiated mass, but rather as two equal, related objects.

Now, clearly, we do not see a complete duplication of part one in part two; only the first four measures of each eight-measure part relate this way. So by making our initial observation we are actually also cutting our two halves into equal subgroups, since the four-measure mark occurs just midway through each section (Ex. 2–3). Despite the primitiveness

Ex. 2-3

```
random level  ·····················································

                          1                    2
first slice   ···················· / ·······················

second slice  ·········/··········//·········/···········
                     a         b        a'        b'
```

of these slices our view of the music is gradually being refined. The labels a and a′ seem appropriate in terms of the identity, and, at this point, b′ relates to b just in the sense that it is an alternative answer to an "a"— that is, some other way to follow a and fill out a larger (two-part) section.

Naturally, then, our attention is called to the relation of b and b′— must they be entirely different just because they are not replicas of each other? We can observe (Ex. 2–4) that both b parts begin by resembling each other to a large extent. Both regions begin with a steady succession of half notes; the direction in the second case is the reverse of the first,

Ex. 2-4

but the shape (four steps in a straight line) is the same, and, moreover, both lines start with the same note in the same register (D). This imitation does not continue after measure 14, so we must note that the *first halves* of the b groups are related, suggesting yet another slicing in half (16 measures = 8 + 8 = 4+4+4+4 = 2+2+2+2+2+2+2+2). The fact that the first halves of the 4-measure b groups relate more closely than do the second halves corresponds to the original observation that the first halves of the 8-measure sections are more closely related than are the second halves. This last level of continuity (blocks of two measures each) aligns fairly well with overall surface changes: note the places where eighth notes give way to quarter notes, half notes to eighth notes, etc.

Once again we are faced with two compared sections, each growing out of two closely related sections: measures 7–8 (answering 5–6) and measures 15–16 (answering 13–14, the counterpart of 5–6). As mentioned, the imitation of shape no longer holds. But the rhythm (where the notes fall, and how long they last) of measure 15 closely resembles that of measure 7, so once again a loose relation between segments is seen. At this point, we can safely follow the four subsections as a succession of familiar events, for we can now see how all of b' relates to all of b, just as all of a' simply *equals* all of a.

Thus far our notion of this music is limited to equal amounts of time articulated by various degrees of identity: total duplication, inversional imitation, rhythmic similarity. We can, however, get more involved with the specific notes that articulate these identities by trying to relate some of the pitch shapes to each other, as we did in chapter 1. A convenient place to start is the shape identified as yielding a striking inversion in the opposite half of the piece: the four-step straight line of measures 5–6. This shape, made here out of the slowest moving notes of the music, appears also in the first instance of the fastest notes, the eighth notes of measure 2 (Ex. 2–5). This segment, which isolates itself by virtue of the slower notes before and after it (our slice includes the downbeat A of

Ex. 2-5

measure 3 because the eighth-note rhythm includes the attack of that note, which is only heard as being longer *after* it has begun to sound), can be described as four step points moving in a straight line, and as such appears as a diminution of the half-note shape.

Let us next consider the two notes phrased together in measure 4 (Ex. 2–6). It is reasonable to hear this detail (which is clearly separable

Ex. 2-6

by virtue of the slur mark, the preceding repeated notes, and the following larger skip) as being related to our straight shape. In a piece that accustoms us to dividing things in half, the two step points are easily seen as half of the four notes we have chosen as the "original" or generating shape (Ex. 2–7).

Ex. 2-7

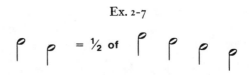

Recalling now that so much of what happens in part one reappears in some form (exactly or imitated) in part two, we can see that a good deal of the surface activity can be "accounted for" by this general shape notion; much of measures 2, 3, 4, 5, 6, 10, 11, 12, 13, and 14 can be "read" in this way, and this reading forms a kind of counterpoint with the more regular, measured progression of equal time units (our initial slicing of the music). Each path of continuity proceeds within the context of the other.

Meanwhile, what of the remaining music, the gaps between these relatable shapes? In particular, the music does not even begin with an instance of this shape. Here we must make a choice: we can force all the music into a succession of instances of this shape, or we can see if some second shape can be useful to describe some of the remaining pitch gestures. Consider measure 1, for example (Ex. 2–8). Insisting that our

Ex. 2-8

straight shape be an index of all gestural form in this piece, we could view this first motion as an ascending step pair followed by a descending pair (Ex. 2–9). But the rhythm hardly suggests such a view, with the

Ex. 2-9

relative durations and metrical positions of the four notes tending to associate the two middle pitches together. Our continuing with this insistence may make some of the piece look silly, or poorly composed.

On the other hand, we can define measure 1 (we include the measure 2 downbeat because the length of that note, compared to the previous three notes, suggests the completion of a gesture at that point) as a shape in its own right. Then the measure 1 shape appears as a useful contrast to the straight shape—it is a bent shape, changing direction in the middle. Perhaps we can think of it as a step in one direction followed by a skip in the other, or as two steps in opposite directions separated by a skip.[1] Any description that helps us see relations between this segment and others in the music can serve as our definition.

We can, in fact, read out many of the gaps in terms of this bent shape.

1. This kind of generalizing is often critically useful in analysis. By tying ourselves to a rigid definition or description of a musical event, a description that merely reproduces verbally all the information presented by the fragment, we may rob ourselves of the chance to see related but varied versions of the original. Note how we fared with our straight shape by thinking of it as "steps in one direction" rather than, more strictly, "descending steps." The latter description would obscure even the relation between the two prime instances of the shape, measures 5–6 and 13–14.

After the introduction of the bent shape in the first measure, the next music that doesn't seem to relate to the straight shape occurs in measure 7 (the measure 3 repetitions being thought of as shapeless, or neutral). These three eighth notes describe this bent shape, a skip in one direction followed by a step in the other direction (this being a backwards version of the generalized shape of the first measure). And measure 8, which closes part one, can be thought of as a straightening out of this shape, since it presents a third followed by a step in the *same* direction. In fact (and perhaps significantly, in view of its position at the end of the section), the figure in measure 8 looks like a combination of the features of both straight and bent shapes: the intervals of the bent shape, the direction pattern of the straight shape. We can think of this item as a kind of summary of the two kinds of surface gestures we have seen in the first half of the piece.

The eighth notes in measure 15 constitute the only other real gap in our straight-shape reading, and this figure too resembles our bent shape. So we can read the entire piece, at this primitive level, as a succession of two kinds of things, both of which are introduced really in the first two measures (or, alternatively, are introduced at the starting points of the first two four-measure blocks, thus intersecting significantly with our other, i.e., time-unit mode of continuity). In this sense we can see the piece as growing out of its own first events. Ex. 2–10 presents a summary of this pathway through the music (with "b" = bent shape, "s" = straight shape).

Ex. 2-10

```
m. 1  2  3  4  5  6  7  8  9  10 11 12 13 14 15 16
   b......s ...... s ... s..........b.. s+b..b........s........s.....s............ b .....
```

Now, though we may find these ways of looking at the piece interesting, we haven't approached the essential matter of the music, the pitches; and though we may hear these pitches in terms of, or projected by, the various paths of shapes or blocks of measures, we haven't begun to deal with the all-important musical information they carry.

In the composition of the previous chapter we found the triad to be the common reference for both linear and harmonic activity. A quick scan of this theme will show that the D triad (that is, just a transposition of the structure underlying the previous piece) is very much in evidence.

The first and last notes, the highest (in the original version, where the last D is an octave higher) and lowest notes are members of the D triad. The D triad is immediately spelled out as the succession of the first three downbeats (Ex. 2–11). These are also the longest notes of the three-

Ex. 2-11

measure span (here recalling that the repeated A of measure three essentially represents four beats' worth of A, according to the rearticulation notion established in chapter 1). The D triad notes also serve as first–last and highest–lowest boundaries for this first three-measure span, and as first–last and lowest boundaries for the first complete four-measure unit. Similar evidence of the prominence of the D triad is found throughout.

But, concentrating for the moment on the first four-bar unit, we know that the D triad provides only a few of the notes of the passage, and we need to see if, with the D triad as *reference*, we can interpret the nontriad notes. (In chapter 1 all notes, whether members of the C triad or not, were referred to—that is, derived their meaning from—the C triad). A convenient place to start is the simple repetition of A in measure 3; we know how to interpret this succession from our experience in the previous analysis. But similarly we can regard the move to B (measure 4) and back as a neighbor embellishment. So the entire second half of the first four-bar unit reduces to (embellishes) A, a member of the D triad.

Working backward, we find the next earlier important note (longer than its neighbors) is D. Between this D and the boundary A we see a series of faster (less important) notes; obviously, they serve to connect these two triad stations. That is, E, F♯, and G are understood as carriers of motion from one triad place to another. In short, they are passing tones. We should note that the metrical orientation of these notes (on weak beats, or not on beats at all) suggests (or "inflects" them for) their passing function, as does their comparative brevity.

Since the initial F♯ in the first measure is "its own excuse," we need only interpret the other two notes of measure 1 in order to have a complete reading of the four-bar unit in terms of the triad. We can start by studying the E, the easier note to interpret. Since it occurs on a weak beat (as compared to the surrounding notes on strong beats), and since it is short (compared to the relative length of the F♯ and D), we can view the E as a passing tone from the F♯ to the D. It may at first seem strange that a passing tone can carry motion over an interruption (the G), but such situations (embedded as they are in more complicated surfaces) immediately create interest, because they are not obvious. If we restrict our search for such relations to the immediately adjacent, we limit our ability to appreciate a multidimensional structure. The acceptance of such intriguingly nondirect motions will prove to be a very powerful tool for rich analytic understanding. We must be sure, however, not to lift out notes haphazardly, and then connect them into a simple line; we are, it must be remembered, verbalizing what our hearing senses, and so we must choose such connections on the basis of promptings from (generally) rhythm (that is, meter and duration). Finally, it should be noted that this interpretation, of E as passing from F♯ to D, is made more plausible in this context because the *other* pair of triad tones (the D and A previously discussed) is also connected by passing tones.

We now come to the stickier problem of interpreting the remaining nontriad note of measure 1, the G. A possible explanation, suggested at least by the functions of all the other nontriad tones in the passage, is that it, too, is a passing tone. Consider that F♯, as initiator of the music, is the repository of multiple triadic power, and that its energy splits off now in two directions at once: down, through E, to the long, accented D; and up, through G, to the elaborated, accented A of measure 3. This may be a more disturbing interpretation than our view of the E, since E was close to both triad elements in the motion, while G is far from its goal (we must hold on to the G, suspend our expectation of resolution of the nontriad note into its goal, a triad note). But perhaps this is just why the G is placed on a relatively strong beat (as opposed to the completely weak E)—G receives a certain extra emphasis (though yet definitely weaker than F♯ and A, the posts of the motion) and we can mark its entry, and thus retain its sound, more readily. And perhaps this is also why the goal of this upward motion, the A, is treated so elaborately (given two full measures of embellishment); the elaboration of A tends to confirm and strengthen the arrival. We now have a satisfactory pic-

Ex. 2-12

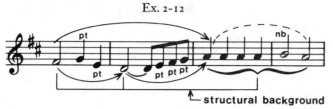

— structural background

ture of the passage, with the three downbeat triad notes interconnected by step (Ex. 2–12). And this diagram can be reduced as in Ex. 2–13.

Ex. 2-13

We see now how the first four-bar unit, half of the first section of the piece, is an elaborate expression of its own home-base triad, the D triad; and while this painstaking discovery still does not constitute analysis (in the sense that it just describes materials and how they are used, but doesn't yet portray the special kind of pitch story that we expect a tonal piece to tell), such a full understanding of the passage will help when we need to put this link into perspective in the larger context of the entire "piece."[2]

At this point, and before going on to perform similar analytic investigations on the other four-bar segments and then to paste these results together into a more unified picture, it may do well to review what we have concluded about this first four-bar unit in a special way: we will build up, as opposed to breaking down.

Imagine, as a first, germinal stage, just the D triad:

stage 1 :   A

F#

D

---

2. Such understanding, and particularly the ordered scheme that follows, is not meant to indicate the way Haydn actually composed such a passage. Our business, as analysts, is with the presented music and how we may find it coherent. The relation between Haydn and his music may well be of great interest, but lies in another domain of investigation (such as the historical, social, or psychological).

This would constitute the extreme conceptual background for the four-bar unit.

The triad is then "arpeggiated" into a form that the passage seems to follow:

$$\text{stage 2:} \quad \begin{matrix} & & A \\ F\# & \cdots\cdots & \\ & & D \end{matrix}$$

Already we see the F♯ splitting off and moving both to the A and the D; so next we need to supply passing tones to carry this motion:

$$\text{stage 3:} \quad F\# \begin{matrix} \nearrow G \longrightarrow A \\ \searrow E \searrow \\ \qquad\qquad D \end{matrix}$$

Next, since we know that the D goal is reached before the A goal, we can now arpeggiate what we had diagrammed as a simultaneous A–D interval:

$$\text{stage 4a:} \quad F\# \begin{matrix} \nearrow G \longrightarrow A \\ \searrow E \\ \qquad \searrow D \end{matrix}$$

And then similarly arpeggiate what was originally diagrammed as a simultaneous passing interval:

$$\text{stage 4b:} \quad \begin{matrix} & & G & & & A \\ F\# & & & & & \\ & & & E & & \\ & & & & D & \end{matrix}$$

This shape begins to resemble our tune quite closely. All we need do now is fill in the D–A gap with passing tones:

$$\text{stage 5:} \quad \begin{matrix} & & G & & & & & G & A \\ F\# & & & & & & F\# & & \\ & & & E & & E & & & \\ & & & & D & & & & \end{matrix}$$

At a sixth stage, or during stages 4 or 5, we can rearticulate the A and insert a neighbor tone (B) to form the A elaboration that ends the unit. Then all these notes get rhythmicized in a way appropriate to their functions; the result is the passage. It may be instructive to play each of these stages in order.

As we move into the second four-bar unit we first encounter the descending step motion that prompted a description of the music in terms of such shapes. But now, in terms of our D triad as basic reference, we can see that this descending motion starts, appropriately, on a triad pitch (D), and descends to another triad station (A); of course we think of this A (measure 6) as a momentary resting place because it is longer than the preceding steps in the figure. Once again, then, we have an interval of the D triad arpeggiated and filled in by passing tones.

The next pitch is G, which we might be tempted to regard as another passing tone on the way down to the next triad station. But the rhythm suggests that not this G, but the next one (on beat 3) is the receiver of motion from the measure 6 A; *this* G does pass then to F♯, the next triad pitch; and in this overall descent from D to F♯, the eighth notes of measure 7, being so much shorter and faster than the previous or following steps in the line, seem like a momentary retracing, a slowing down of the descending motion (and done in such a way as to invoke the image of the shape of the opening measure) (Ex. 2–14).[3] Perhaps to balance this

Ex. 2-14

delaying tactic, the scale now speeds up (quarter-note motion, rather than the earlier half-note motion). And if we are confused about the hidden, or not entirely clear, motion from A to F♯ (measure 6 to the end of measure 7), then the skip in measure 8, just from A to F♯, seems to clarify or summarize the recent progress of the large descending scale pattern.

But our grand scale does not stop at F♯ (which, because it is a triad pitch, would be an appropriate or satisfying stopping point); by the end of beat 2 of measure 8 F♯ is still the most recent point of progress in the downward motion, and F♯ now moves to E. E of course is a nontriad pitch, and so we may expect it to pass on to the next triad station, D. But

3. The rhythm prevents us from hearing the measure 7 sequence A–G–B–A as a double-neighbor embellishment of A, even though A, as a triad pitch and as the basic point of reference in the vicinity, might warrant such fancy treatment. But the length and placement of the beat 3 G calls much more attention to it than to the beat 2 A.

it fails to do this, for E is also the last pitch of part one, the pitch that is followed by the unique silence that demarcates the ending of a major portion of the total statement. Our overall scalar descent, then, is from the D of measure 5 to this E at the end of part one, and the clarifying A–F♯ skip in measure 8 can additionally be seen as another retracing (like that of measure 7), which interrupts or slows down this descent.

These interruptions aside, the single-minded purpose of the second four-bar unit of part one is this incomplete scale from D to E. Thus, while the first segment of part one just exposes its own triad, the second segment raises an issue: what will happen to this nontriad E? Will the scale ever reach the low D, its apparent goal? Will E simply turn around and move back to its progenitor, F♯? In sum, the first four bars are stable, and the second unstable. This pairing, with the unstable segment second, renders the entire part one unstable, since it ends up on the nontriad E. In fact, we can view the overall progress of the phrase as moving from the *first* F♯ to the last E, so that the larger but more local descent from high D to E is seen as a parenthesized motion inside the more encompassing descent from F♯; the imagined or expected goal of both motions is middle D (Ex. 2–15).

Ex. 2-15

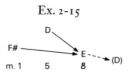

We can also at this point see the overall function of part two: to conclude what part one has set up, but failed to accomplish—locally, a resolution of the E; but more generally a completion of the expected large-scale succession F♯–E–D. Notice that this most general description of the music is presaged by the very first completed motion, from the initial F♯ through E to the D of measure 2. The last two notes of part one, F♯–E, succinctly summarize the basic motion so far.

If part one has failed to deal conclusively with this E,[4] can't part two

---

4. It must be emphasized that we are dealing strictly with the melody in isolation here. It was previously warned that the missing lines would certainly add other information. In particular E may, in the linear sense, be an unresolved nontriad note, but, simultaneously and just as realistically, be a *triad* note of a new, local harmony (see chapter 1). Certainly we see hints of the A triad here—the emphasis on A in measures 6–8, the A–E span in measure 8.

resolve the matter efficiently in one or two notes? After all, in an immediate sense, this E does seem to return into the triad—the very next note, the first of part two, is the neighboring F♯, which can adequately receive the E; and, perhaps more satisfactorily, D is actually reached on the downbeat of measure 10, thus completing the descent. But, on the other hand, the descent from F♯ to E has taken 8 measures, and we expect an equal amount of time to be devoted to a retreatment of this issue. The fact that E does locally resolve into F♯ or D is countered by the fact that, quite literally, the music *starts again* in measure 9; it picks up in exact imitation of the beginning, as if to try once more to move F♯ through E into D.

And now we must face the problem of the fragmentary status of this "piece." For if we expect part two to pick up here, restate the initial music, and complete the motion left incomplete in part one, we will be disappointed (and of course this failure of part two to complete the motion serves to motivate the whole symphony movement to continue past these initial 16 bars).

And we are disappointed most cruelly: for Haydn raises our hopes by starting out in the same way, proceeding familiarly for four measures, but then taking leave of this register altogether; starting with the D of measure 13 he brings us *up* instead of down, and we seem to get farther from our goal. It is all the more interesting that this escape takes the form of a direct, teasing imitation of the "cooperative" figure of measures 5–6, and at a corresponding point in the phrase!

And while thus frustrating our expectations from the previous 12 measures, the last four-bar group produces further problems. What is the goal of this rising four-note motion? It seems to reach G, a nontriad note that itself does not resolve into the triad. The succession G–F♯–G–E in measure 15 is easy to deal with; the rhythm and shape of the first three notes suggest that F♯ is locally a neighbor to G (which thus "lasts" for 1½ beats), and this succession reduces to G–E. Since D is then the next note, the succession is G–E–D, reminiscent of that succession an octave lower at the beginning of the music. But *there* the G had a function: to carry motion from F♯ up to A in the initial exposure of the triad.

It is, in fact, only in a complete line that we can expect to see the resolution both of overall motions *and* of smaller details. In this sense, as the music of chapter 1 was too static, this fragment is too active, giving rise to expectation that is not treated to resolution within the local time-span we have studied. These issues of expectation, development, and resolution are crucial—perhaps unique—to the tonal system. And so, with experience in the analysis of tune-lines gained, and with expectations raised, we turn now to a complete melody line.

ꭗꭗꭗꭗꭗꭗꭗꭗꭗ **3**

Analysis of a Complete Melody by Corelli

The analytic work of chapter 2 proceeded on a less primitive level than that of chapter 1; the ability to make discriminations and recognize relations on what can be described as a "pretriadic" level was *assumed* in the second chapter, having been developed as a way of thinking and approaching material in the first chapter. Similarly, such "post-triadic" relations as the neighbor-note formation or the passing function, or, indeed, the very notion that the triad *is* the referential background for a tonal passage, need no longer be "discovered," but can be used as tools for more complex observations and syntheses. Each analysis can build on the understanding won in previous attempts; eventually, for example, it would not be necessary even to spell out the exact deployment of the triad in an obvious and straightforward triadic tune. In this way longer and more involved compositions can be studied successfully. At the same time, such a progression of analyses will have the result that, for each piece, we will be saying less and less about what that piece shares with all other tonal pieces (such as that it *is* demonstrably triadic), and more about what is unique to that piece (for instance, just *how* it is triadic in its own way: in short, how it makes a piece out of itself).

Meanwhile we moved ahead from the previous chapter, in which we viewed a portion of a melody as making progress toward a presumed

Ex. 3–1

goal. The melody presented for study in Ex. 3–1, the violin line of the Sarabande movement of the Sonata for Violin and Cembalo by Corelli (opus 5, #8), can more satisfactorily be considered a complete piece. At least we are guilty of only *one* kind of artificial detaching—of the melody from its harmonic context. We can expect to hear completed structures within the linear triadic context that we are learning to construct for our hearing.

Many kinds of identities are present to suggest a first carving of the music into units. An interesting way to begin is with the first detail, which describes a rhythm that keeps appearing throughout:

It is natural to hear this detail in isolation since the length of the second note imposes a certain pause at that point. The reappearance of this rhythm in measure 5 and its immediate duplication in measure 7 *with the same pitches* reinforce the separability of this detail. Listening for it throughout, then, we find, among other things, that it occurs at the beginning of every four measures: measures 1, 5, 9, 13, 17, and 21 all begin with this figure in the identical metrical orientation. Then there are other instances of this rhythm: measures 7, 11, and 19 present this figure the same way, and these points all split four-measure groups (as already grouped by the first list of such figures) into two-measure sub-groupings. This observation produces a string of measures with familiar signposts every two measures, with gaps only at measures 3, 15, and 23. But notice (Ex. 3–2) that the rhythm that begins measure 3 resembles very closely this rhythmic motive: the quarter note is split into two

Ex. 3–2

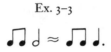

The added eighth note can be seen to function as a "rhythmic passing tone," a connector of two more fundamental points.

eighths. And the other two gaps, measures 15 and 23, present essentially the same rhythm as measure 3: the dotted quarter is lengthened to a half note. In fact, the rhythm in measure 15 is not heard as different from that of measure 3 until the *end* of the measure comes (that is, after the motion part of the figure is complete and already recognized) and no pitch is struck on the final eighth of the measure (Ex. 3–3).

Ex. 3–3

So our music proceeds in two-measure units organized into four-measure groups, and the effect of this particular rhythmic motive is to place a certain emphasis on the second beat of each initial measure. On the one hand this may just be a characteristic of sarabandes, but, more interestingly, it tells us something about how to regard pitches that occur on these unusually stressed second beats. We will recall this advice when we are in a position to examine the pitches closely. But meanwhile it should be obvious that it is hardly possible to observe the steady progression of this original (two-note) rhythmic motive without noticing the pitches and intervals the rhythm articulates. In all cases but measures 5 and 7, the rhythm describes an ascending perfect fourth. The two exceptions are descending perfect fifths, the complementary interval. The relation between these two directions and sizes becomes explicit when we see the version of measure 11, E–A, duplicate the pitch content of that of measure 5. But the instance in measure 5 (the second occurrence in the music) is already closely related to the original, germinal instance, B–E, since the pitch E is shared (and in the same register). In fact, these two pitch pairs, B–E and A–E, account for almost all occurrences of this rhythm. The only exceptions, in measures 9 and 19, also feature such sharings: the F♯–B of measure 9 shares B with the original, and the A–D of measure 19 shares A with the E–A form. Curiously, all these fourths are

fourths away from each other: if we transpose the original B–E up a
fourth (that is, transpose it by the measurement of its own interval, or build
a *chain* of fourths), the result is the next example in the music, E–A. If
we transpose this original B–E *down* a fourth, the result is F♯–B. Finally
the A–D is won by transposing the original up an additional fourth (Ex.
3–4).

Ex. 3–4

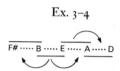

    This kind of slicing, fascinating as it may be (and it is particularly
rich as a kind of counterpoint to whatever other kinds of paths we discover) does not yet succeed in carving the music into fundamental units
of *progression*: we are left with an even unfolding of two- and four-
measure groupings, as marked by the figures we have been studying. But
a division at the next larger (eight-measure) level is also suggested by
events in the music, and it is at this level that we can begin to grasp the
overall design of the piece. At the end of eight measures (that is, after
two four-measure units), a special item appears: for the first time, we
have a three-beat note (B, measure 8). Eight measures later another such
point comes about (B, measure 16), and finally E in the last measure of the
piece concludes this succession of longest values that carves the total
duration into three equal areas (which we can call 1, 2, and 3).
    Many aspects of the music quickly come to mind to support this
division. First of all, there are only three such long (full-measure) notes,
and the final one is the last note of the piece. This suggests a kind of
closing function to the long note, and, in retrospect (or on rehearing),
we can hear the prior two instances as endings also. Second, the repeats
in the music (not, of course, the visual appearance of repeat signs, but the
overall sense of large-scale repetition that results in performance) match
these punctuation placements; for it is just the stretch of the music from
the beginning to this first (measure 8) long note that is heard twice
in succession, and then the remainder of the music is heard twice. This
suggests that we think of the first of our three regions as a separate
section, followed by regions 2 and 3 as a second section. The piece, then,
most basically splits into two uneven sections (measures 1–8, 9–24). And
finally (and this is not a complicated observation, since it relates so

closely to literal repetition), the music from measure 17 to the end is a repeat of the eight bars that precede it *transposed down a fifth.* (It is this device, for example, that turns the F♯–B of measure 9 back into the B–E of measure 17, since upward transposition by a fourth is equivalent to downward transposition by a fifth).

In sum, then, the succession of longest notes carves the piece into two major sections, and splits the second (larger) one into two related parts. It seems best to refer to these large-scale divisions as section 1, section 2a (that is, measures 9–16) and section 2b.

Now, as with our observations on the initial rhythmic motive figure, we can hardly hear these long notes without also realizing the pitch information carried by them. For the succession of them is B–B–E, a projection into the largest scale of our original motivic detail, B–E (with the notes in the correct order also, but with the ascending fourth converted into a descending fifth, a transformation that the original detail itself undergoes over the course of its regular reappearances). Furthermore, the end points of the two fundamental sections describe in even greater summary B–E. And since these are also the first two notes of the piece, we can immediately see that B is the first and last note of section 1, that B to E is the overall progression of the music (from first to last note), and that this progression is immediately foreshadowed by the first separable detail of the piece. The progression takes on a particularly gradual shape in that the opening B seems to be retained through its reappearance in measure 8 and again in measure 16, finally to connect to E at the end. But notice that this connection, so long delayed, is explicit in the music: the last five notes of the piece are just B–A–G–F♯–E, a joining of the first and last notes of the music by intervening scalar steps (passing tones). And this quick descent grows immediately out of a local reference to the original, generating B–E interval (Ex. 3–5).

Ex. 3–5

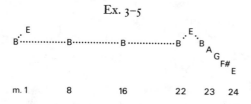

This 24-measure journey fits our two-section view as follows: section 1 seems to be the area that establishes the pitch B (notice particularly the way the final B in measure 8 is preceded by a unique anticipation figure, one that has the effect of confirming or announcing B as an important note); and section 2 is then the section that, after prolonging the primacy of B, brings it down through the e-minor scale to its goal, E (notice how section 2 announces itself as a fundamentally new region: the F♯–B version of the original rhythmic detail is the first instance of this rhythm that conforms to the original ascending-fourth shape, the two intervening examples being descending-fifth imitations).

With spectacular swiftness an overall *tonal* view of the music has emerged from some simple, primitive divisions of the surface into related groupings of equal amounts of time as suggested by the simple identities of unique events (the initial detail, the three long notes). Using this journey as a framework we can now delve into the detailed deployment of the notes throughout. This framework, of course, is a particular journey *through the e-minor triad*. The goal of the motion is E, the tonic. The overall span is B–E, the defining, skeletal fifth of the e-minor triad. And the connecting tones are drawn from the e-minor scale. So the full complement of fundamental tonal constructs is established over the course of the piece, and is available for reference at specific points throughout.

Local linear motion at the start of the music is initiated not by the B, which is immediately left by skip, but by the E. The notes that follow it are not easy to interpret. F♯, immediately following E, is rhythmicized in such a way as to seem like a passing tone or a neighbor note, but neither a G nor an E appears to complete the motion. Rather, E's other neighbor, D♯, appears on the next downbeat, and thus carries so much weight that the first motion clearly seems to be in that direction: from E down to D♯. Note that, like the D♯, the initial E is stressed (here we call upon our observation of the general condition of second-beat stresses in regularly spaced places).

This D♯ is either a passing tone, on the way down to the next triad station, or a neighbor note to the generating E. Since the next note (end of measure 2) is again E, we may be tempted to regard the entire succession E–F♯–D♯–E as an elaborate E-embellishment (a double-neighbor formation). But, whether or not this second E is capable of absorbing the unresolved F♯, it can hardly be thought of as a resolution of the D♯. The metrical position of the D♯, combined with its long duration, renders that note so powerful in contrast to the E that we are not likely to arrive at this interpretation naturally, and would only accept this mode of hearing the notes if there were absolutely no more satisfactory pathway.[1]

An alternative may be provided by the next downbeat, C, whose presence allows us to connect a series of stressed notes in a straight line: E of measure 1, D♯ of measure 2, C of measure 3.[2] This C even moves on to B, the receiving triad station; but here the rhythm is quite clear: we must regard B as a neighbor to C, and the entire third measure is obviously C's domain. It is in the fourth measure that C finally descends to B and comes momentarily to rest there. To this point, then, the music seems to jump from B to E, and then to descend gradually back down. This motion occupies one of our four-measure units.

The second unit begins with another high E (which, with the preceding B, sums up the previous motion by restating the interval obliquely). This E seems to serve several functions. First, it makes reference to the starting point of the downward motion, which seems to continue with the next note; second, it seems to punctuate that continued motion by interrupting it at a significant point (after one link, E to B, has been completed); and finally, since it is the strongest E we have had so far, it may at last be the note we need to claim the straying F♯ of measure 1.

Clearly the descending motion continues after this interruption, for not only does the A of measure 5 pick up directly from the B of the preceding measure, but it descends to G, the next step, in precisely the same way that C recently descended into B (Ex. 3–6). This sequence device is useful not only in calling our attention to the parallelism of

---

1. Normal rhythmic embodiment of the neighbor formation would consist of a succession that emphasizes the neighbored pitch and deemphasizes the neighbor itself (through a combination of metrical and durational means):

$$\frac{3}{4} \quad \text{♩ (C)} \quad \text{♩ (B)} \mid \text{♩. (C)}$$

For a double-neighbor group this might take the form

$$\text{♩ (C)} \quad \text{♫ (D B)} \mid \text{♩. (C)}$$

2. It might be objected that such descending motions should avoid the overly large augmented-second skip D♯–C; in fact, the minor mode usually behaves in such a way as to contract this dissonant (skip-sized) step into a whole step. This passage, if heard in this way, would seem to be an exception. (But see footnote 3 for an alternative.)

Ex. 3–6

these two movements, but also in establishing the relationship between B (of measure 4) and G (of measure 6): both are triad stations, both resting points in the scalar descent. To articulate further the sense of arrival at G (which is not a stressed note like the B), the stepwise motion halts at that point (Ex. 3–7).

Ex. 3–7

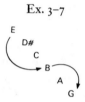

If this descent from E to G, spanning an interval of the e-minor triad (and carved into two e-minor-triad intervals by the B), has been difficult to follow, the composer simply sums up the long-range motion by stating just the outline of it succinctly in the very next notes (Ex. 3–8).

Ex. 3–8

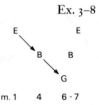

But this descent to G, along with the immediately following summary that clarifies that descent, does not conclude section 1, for the music turns around and begins to climb back up (a direction already suggested by the ascending clarification of measures 6–7). The A of measure 7 is a passing tone from the G of the previous measure to the final (anticipation-confirmed) B, which brings the entire section to rest. We must recast, now, our overall sense of the accomplishment of section 1; the motion from E to G, after all, does not actually *start* the music, but is preceded by B. Since we return to B at the end of the section, we must hear the E–G motion as parenthesized inside the larger (structurally sustained) B (Ex. 3–9).[3]

Ex. 3–9

B(E ⟶ G) B

m.1 1   6   8

So, in the most general sense, section 1 establishes B *as a member of* the e-minor triad. It is this firm e-minor B that is being prepared for ultimate descent to the tonic E at the end of section 2 (the end of the piece).

Section 2 begins (measure 9) with B well established, and presumably ready to descend. But this descent does not take place, as we know, until the very end of the music. What happens to delay that descent? To answer this question we must refine our understanding of this section of the piece.

We already know that section 2 establishes itself as an entirely new area: the unique long B of the previous measure, the repeat of the preceding music, the move into a higher register, the closely (closer than previously) imitating shape in measure 9, all contribute to this impression. It almost seems as if the rising F♯ of measure 1, which caused us such interpretative difficulty initially, sets up this higher music of section 2; for the new music *starts* with this F♯, and, in imitating the initial detail of measure 1, completes a symmetrical structure that may be implied by measure 1 (Ex. 3–10). At any rate, the comparison is instructive because

Ex. 3–10

```
                        B
        E  F#     F#
   B                
                       (B E  F# B)

m. 1           9
```

3. An alternative interpretation, which does not, however, alter the overall picture of the section, would follow an insistence on denying a step connection between D♯ and C (measure 2–3). If we heard those opening notes as a neighbor group around E, then the elaborate C of measure 3 is a long-range neighbor to the opening B, with that neighbor formation closing in measure 4. In this case, the parenthesized element is this large E-embellishment; and the overall motion is B (m. 1)–C–B (m. 4)–A–G (m. 6) and back—that is, also a grand prolongation of B over section 1, with B established *as a member of* the e-minor triad, and in preparation for its ultimate descent through the e-minor scale to E at the close of the music.

F♯ is just a neighboring tone in measure 1, but is here in measure 9 a part of the fundamental fourth figure. This figure in measure 1 defined the overall fundamental interval of the music, and here in its measure 9 transposition it is likely to carry much significance. In fact, if we notice the B–F♯ outline spanned by the section division (measures 8–9, the first and last notes at the juncture), as well as the B octave outlined over these two measures, we get a strong impression of the b triad. We must see, then, whether we want to continue interpreting the oncoming notes according to the old e triad or to the b triad we are beginning to notice here.

We are aided in our attempt to study the notes of these measures by the appearance of a sequence: the rhythm-pitch shape of measures 9–10 is duplicated a step lower in measures 11–12. Just as the use of sequence in section 1 (measures 3–6) applies to a long-range scalar descent, so does it here. But first we can notice that the very form chosen for the embodiment of this sequence is particularly appropriate to this piece. The rhythm of measure 1 is reproduced in measure 9, and the rhythm of measure 3 reappears in measure 10. So the new sequence is a sewing together of two rhythmic events of the earlier music; as such, it is less arbitrary, more significant (Ex. 3–11). The pitch shapes assigned to these

Ex. 3–11

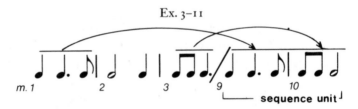

The rhythms of measures 1 and 3 seem easy to lift out and combine since those two downbeats form posts in the two-measure level of continuity.

rhythms are similarly derived from section 1. The pitch shape of the measure 10 rhythm is just that of the pitch shape of the *source* of that rhythmic detail (measure 3); and the pitch form of measure 9 relates closely to that of measure 1: the former ascending fourth followed by a step in the same direction has now become a similar fourth followed by a step in the opposite direction (we already know to relate the two fourths, as well as, originally, the *rhythm* of the two fourths).

The sequence describes a scalar descent, but it is not immediately clear which scale is being followed. We have previously been drawing on the e-minor scale (the proper environment for the e-minor triad), but now have a strong feeling of the B triad (its mode is actually not certain with just the information provided by the violin line; but the tonic quality of B—that is, thinking of B now as root of its own triad, rather than as fifth of the e-minor triad—is strongly suggested by the way B is presented in measure 8). The initial notes of descent in measures 9 and 10 could come equally well from the e-minor scale or the b-minor scale (remembering the behavior of the upper portion of minor scales).[4] Locally, the rhythm suggests the A of measure 9 as a passing tone, and the F♯ of measure 10 as a neighbor tone; at this point, then, the music seems to span the e-minor interval B–G, and the scale may as well be that of e. But the next unit of the sequence, measures 11–12, brings the overall descent to F♯, thus describing the interval B–F♯ (from measure 9 to measure 12), an interval of the b triad. The confusion may actually be a strong point here, rather than a detraction, since, if we eventually feel that the music here establishes the primacy of the b triad (B as tonic), then the transition from one tonic and triad as reference to another will have been gracefully gradual rather than abrupt.

It is this larger descent, from the initial B (measure 9) to the F♯ of measure 12, that seems convincing: for the sequence stops here (hence a feeling of accomplishment at this point), and the overall B–F♯ descent fills in the initial F♯–B skip (just as, in section 1, the initial B–E skip is recomposed into a gradual E–B descent by step).

The next measure (measure 13) is quite a rich one, and plays into our developing sense of changing triad reference very skillfully. The F♯–B over the bar line describes the b triad and refers to the interval arpeggiated in the preceding descent; but the B–E of measure 13 refers to the e triad—indeed, it repeats the opening detail of the piece. (The pitch B as shared element between the two triads is made explicit in this juncture.) Meanwhile, we can see the E as the next step down from the F♯ of measure 12 (especially since we saw things this way with the A

4. The close resemblance of the contents of the two scales is of course just an instance of the general closeness of fifth-related scales, and even by itself can help justify a move from e minor to b minor. And the fact that the fifth of one such scale is the root of the other (as made explicit by the comparison of measures 1 and 9) is another theoretical advantage to the standard compositional move.

in measure 5), and the downbeat B as just an interrupting reference to the new tonic (we did this too, with the E in measure 5). In fact we can see the B–E interval as representing the e triad while simultaneously viewing each of the notes making up that interval as significant in the world of the b triad. Finally, to make matters even more richly complicated, if we are now connecting the E of measure 13 to the descent from B in measure 9, then the overall progress to this point is B–E, once again an interval of the e triad (with all the materials still possibly deriving from the e scale)![5]

Measure 14 finally clarifies this intriguing confusion. The rather startling dissonant interval from E to A♯ (over the bar line) calls our attention to this first non-e-minor pitch, the function of which is clearly to act as a leading tone to B, lending that pitch a tonic aspect. It is important to note that this interval is the *first* dissonant interval of the line, and this note is the *only* pitch so far to depart from the e-minor collection.

The succeeding F♯–B intervals (measure 14) further establish the b triad, and all that is left to section 2a is a direct descent from F♯ to B (in measure 16). This long B of course associates with that of measure 8 (hence the original slicing at this point), but now this B is clearly its own tonic (no longer E's dominant). Furthermore, an overall view of section 2a becomes clear: the b-minor scale is now complete (from the B in measure 9 to the lower B in measure 16). At the same time, since F♯ is the first pitch of the section, since that F♯ reappears as the end point of the sequence (measure 12), and since it is F♯ that is directly connected to the tonic B in measure 16 (the immediate descent), then a more fundamental overview of section 2a is just the five-note descent F♯–E–D–C♯–B. (The structure of section 2a, then, appears to be a diminution and transposition of the fundamental structure of the entire piece as first described: the five-note descent from the initial B to the final E, as articulated by the last five notes of the music).

---

5. These fluctuating interpretations (the alternations between interpreting notes as members of e-minor constructs and of b-minor constructs) are one of the richer resources of the tonal system. A similar situation was seen in measures 3–4. Here the note B is locally just a neighbor to C (measure 3), but within one measure B is reestablished as a reference point, with C just a passing tone to it. Even in measure 3 alone B can be understood on more than one level simultaneously (as a fundamental note on the one hand, as a mere neighbor to a locally more important note on the other).

And now we can quite readily understand section 2b, the final eight measures of the piece, for this is the segment that is a fifth-transposition of the preceding eight measures. We know then that these last eight measures will resubstitute the e-minor collection of pitches for the b-minor collection, and will likewise replace the b-minor triad as reference with the original (and overall) e-minor triad. And, of course, the striking tritone dissonance over the measure 21–22 bar line will, as previously, call attention to its upper note, the D♯ that will so strongly help re-tonicize E. And, similarly, the scalar descents within the b triad of section 2a will reappear as descents in the e triad.

We are now in a position to answer our question about the delay in the descent of B (see page 35). For at this point we can refine the picture that shows section 1 setting up B and section 2 bringing B down into E: B first gets reinterpreted as the tonic of the b-minor triad, and then is restored to its position as second-most important note in the e-minor triad. B does not descend until it has stood on its own, in its own right. Having presented itself in that prime light, it then resumes its original place and function and descends quickly and visibly to E to establish the overall, triad-defining interval B–E.

We can even predict much about the harmony now that we have a full understanding of the melody. For surely the line spells out chords as clearly as chordal figurations themselves would, and we can see how the fundamental chordal progression accompanying this line would be E–B–E, a spelling that coincides with the fundamental linear information. This identification of the vertical with the horizontal is no different from what we discovered in our chapter 1 analysis.

Finally, we can compare our results here with our partial results in chapter 2. In the Haydn theme we witnessed the attempt of F♯ to pass through E to D; had this motion been completed, we would have witnessed a long-range arpeggiation of an interval of the home-base triad (F♯–D, of the D triad). This view corresponds to our B-to-E picture of this e-minor composition.

The lack of completion of the structure in the D-major example was suggested as a motivating factor in the continuation of the music; and, with our new experience, we can see what that continuation would be like. In fact, we can consult another familiar D-major example that accomplishes the same general goal. The first phrase of the theme from the last movement of Beethoven's Ninth Symphony (Ex. 3–12) shows

Ex. 3–12

the initial F♯ descending, by the end of the phrase, to E. If this is the start of a motion through E to D, completing the triad interval F♯–D, then an "answer" phrase is needed to accomplish this completion. The matching, succeeding phrase starts the music over again (as does the second phrase in the Haydn example, where the first phrase also accomplishes just this much), and brings the F♯ all the way down (Ex. 3–13). F♯–E–D is the long-range (2-phrase) structure, as well as the independent structure of the second phrase alone, as well as (both locally and as a distinct summary of the whole) the concluding detail.

Ex. 3–13

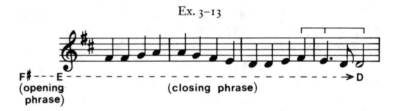

F♯ --- E - →D
(opening   (closing phrase)
phrase)

We have finally witnessed compositional completeness, if in a very primitive and limited way: the Corelli melody is a self-sufficient, satisfying musical statement (even if it forms just one link in a multimovement composition). The statement does not just prolong its own triad (as does the composition of chapter 1), it *moves through it* in a purposeful, goal-directed way. We are now ready to approach a full piece of music, to which we turn in the next chapter.

Analysis of Chopin: Prelude in e minor, Opus 28, No. 4

In studying this piece we are deliberately accelerating our progression toward more complex subjects of analysis. The intention here is to demonstrate the efficacy of the approach developed in the foregoing studies: even leaving portions of this new composition largely unanalyzed, we will find ourselves able to understand a good deal about the music.

It is merely coincidental that this piece begins on the same pitch and occupies the same key, mode, and register as the melody we studied in the last chapter. The real relation between the two compositions (and hence the choice of subject here) lies in the congruence of their overall structures. The Chopin Prelude is simply a more elaborate instance of the structure by which we understood the Corelli melody. Such an insight gives us faith in our analytic abilities and allows us to increase the scope of our investigations. By applying some of the simple modes of understanding won in the first ("chordal") analysis to this composition of exotic, "chromatic" chords, we can learn to approach with confidence any style of tonal composition, without reference to a particular level of theory or harmony study (such as "chromatic harmony") that a consideration of the piece may seem to have as its prerequisite.

The point is not to discover that this piece is "simple," or even easy

to deal with. But the composition does have a melody, and we already
have some successful experience grasping both the overall and the detailed meaning of some tonal melodies. And the total length is no greater
than that of the Corelli melody. As for the chords, which may seem to
be the real prohibitive element, we must recall that we were able, in
chapter 1, to understand the chords of a tonal piece not by virtue of their
names but by a contextual examination of how the chords seemed to
function (how they arise and how they move on).

Finally, the composition is familiar. Good editions are readily available, and one should be chosen to accompany this text. The measures can
be numbered from 1 to 25, and will be referred to freely, as if the score
were reproduced here.

Like the composition of the first chapter, this piece ends in terms of
its beginning: the initial and final chords are e-minor triads. But these two
chords, unlike those of the earlier piece, are not identical. The last one is
in root position, with the tonic pitch on top, while the first one is in a
less definitive (less stable) intervallic arrangement (the $\frac{6}{3}$ inversion), and
has the fifth degree as its melodic note. We have said enough about the
significance of the identity of these two items, and it may be interesting,
within this context of overall home-base assertion, to concentrate on the
minimal *difference* between the two.

First, there is the notion that the final chord rectifies the initial one,
in the sense that it presents the contents of the first chord in "better" form
(root position). Not only is the bass note profitably chosen in the last
chord, but so is the top note (the melody pitch of the chord), for both
these slots display the tonic pitch class, E (hidden in the first chord,
which has E in neither extreme position).

Second, the last chord is physically (spatially) a move down from the
first. Reading from top to bottom, the second, third, and fourth pitches
of the first chord reappear exactly (in the same registral positions) as
the top three pitches of the last chord; but, in addition to this shared
element, the opening chord has only something higher, and the last chord
only something lower (Ex. 4–1). Moreover, the only outstanding element
in chord 1 (the only addition to the shared portion) is B, and the only
addition in the final chord is (various representations of) E. So, quite
literally, B "becomes" E (and this change is succinctly illustrated by the
actual change in melodic notes: B to E).

So within the scope of non-change from first to last chord we actually

Ex. 4–1

see a rather rich *progression*, which apparently takes place over the span of the piece (the first chord becoming the last chord *by way of* all the intervening matter). Because of the unique combination of change and stasis between these two chords, we can actually think of this two-chord relation as a piece by itself! But, less fancifully and more importantly, we can think of the link as a framework for the whole prelude.

Since we now know where we start and what our goal is, it seems useful to survey the outward format of the fabric that connects these two posts. Two striking events suggest a fundamental slicing of the music into sections: a unique total silence in measure 23 divides the piece into a main body and a very brief conclusion; and a less dramatic cessation (the otherwise regular accompaniment halts in measure 12—perhaps in response to which the melody becomes more active than it has been to that point) divides the main body into two fairly equal sections.

A fundamental, form-determining observation follows directly from this slicing, and resembles critical observations from other analyses: just after the central break in measure 12, the music resumes with a repetition of the opening music. The music continues identically, then similarly, and then develops on its own; but the general sense of a "second start," as we have witnessed it before, is clear.

We now have a new level at which to examine first and last chords. We actually have already identified most of these chords, since the first chord of section 1 is just the first chord of the piece; the last chord of section 2 (if we conveniently join the separable cadence at the end to the second section) is of course the last chord of the piece; and the first chord of section 2 must be the same as that of section 1 (because of the repeat that starts there). We need only pin down the last chord of section 1 to add to our original picture of first–last accomplishment. This chord, struck on the downbeat of measure 12, is B^7. So our picture of e (m. 1)– e (m. 25) is refined (Ex. 4–2). That is, the first tonic gets to the last tonic

Ex. 4–2

e   B⁷   e
m. 1   12   25

by way of its dominant; furthermore, this dominant is dissonant (with
the addition of the seventh degree), and is thus an appropriate connector
of the two stabler chords (e minor)—that is, the B chord does not present itself as a place to stay comfortably very long, and tends to push us
toward a resolution. (This resolution comes locally with the pickup of
the repetition, and for the piece as a whole with the arrival of the final
chord).

This general harmonic picture already matches our primitive melodic
frame, for chords of E and B accompany a melody that starts on B and
ends on E. And this melodic journey, from B to E, aligns perfectly well
with the sectional slices that produced that harmonic picture: for if
the music resumes after the break of measure 12, then the B that starts the
melody must be reinstated in measure 13. In fact, it is interesting to see
how this B is emphasized at the start, with the octave jump and the anticipation figure. The wandering figure that connects the two large sections seems just to elaborate on this B-expression (Ex. 4–3). This figure

Ex. 4–3

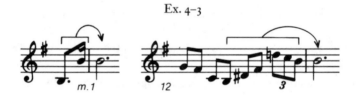

descends to B (the one matching the very first B of the piece) from the
point that it abandons the melody, and then works its way up, around,
and down to the same B-anticipation figure. Furthermore, the figure
seems to fill in the B octave in a way that combines stability and instability: the reference to the B triad following the low B (B–D♯–F♯) makes
a strong, stable element of the pitch-class B, furthering its establishment
up to this point (as in the Corelli melody, where B is tonicized before
it descends to E); and on the other hand, the questionable B/b mode
(the D♯ turns into D♮) and the impatient triplet rhythm that results
directly in the anticipation lend an unstable aspect to the entire expression of B, as if the B were ready to move on (down to E).

These observations, and their coordination with the overall sectional form, suggest we follow the path taken by the initial B. The elaborate anticipation figures set up B as the first note of a gradual scalar descent into the final E (whose quadruple representation in the final chord is the equivalent of the insistent nature of the presentation of B). The descent is easy to follow, since it clearly occupies the foreground of the music and constitutes the essential story of the melody line.

B is the focus of the melodic line in the first four measures: in each of these measures B is the principal note and C is its upper neighbor (because B is three times longer than C and is on the downbeat). In measure 4 B♭ takes the motion down to A, which then establishes itself as the next principal station in the descent. This movement to A is one level removed from normal passing-tone motion, since A itself is probably a scalar passing tone to the next triad station (G); thus B♭ is a *chromatic* passing tone, connecting to scale tones.[1]

That A is the direct heir to B is clear, first of all because it is treated as B was: placed on a downbeat and neighbored by the next upper pitch.[2] But the anticipation device over the bar line between measures 7 and 8 clearly calls to mind the only other such treatment thus far in the music, that of B at the beginning of the piece. It is really at this point that A seems most certainly the next item in a succession of local resting places.

Right after this anticipation-confirmation the descent continues, but A seems to move down to the wrong pitch: if the overall harmonic framework is the e-minor triad, then the scalar connections between B and E, representatives of that triad, should after all be constituents of the e-minor scale. In this sense, G♯ seems like a mistake for G.[3] But when, in the next measure, the G♯ returns to A, we can reinterpret the G♯ as a lower neighbor to A. This is particularly likely in view of the clear a-minor disposition of the notes of both parts in this measure (the bass playing

1. Such a passage demonstrates the analogous relations between tonal constructs at different levels: the tonic is embedded in the tonic triad, the tonic triad in the diatonic collection, and that collection, now, in the total chromatic collection. At any level, elements from the next, more detailed, level can be employed for elaboration of a construct.

2. This situation creates another one of those intriguing tonal ambiguities. B is a principal note in the first four measures but must be reinterpreted as just an embellishing pitch in the second four measures.

3. But moving from A to G♯ can also be heard as justifiable, in the sense that it continues the half-step movement B–B♭–A–G♯. So we wonder if G♯ may bring A to G, as B♭ brought B to A.

the a-minor triad, the first real triad of any consequence since the first measure; the treble describing the same triad in more elaborate fashion). The meandering melody in measure 9, the first such departure from the established format (and apparently an advance notice of the more extensive departure of this type in measure 12, at the fundamental section division), reinforces the sense of the prolongation of A, for, with the a-minor triad as reference, we can interpret the B as a passing tone to the C, the D as an accented, incomplete upper neighbor to the C, and the rest as triad tones.

But the outcome of this digression is F♯, the next long, downbeat pitch. So, in a confusing manner, we seem to have moved from B to A and by now to F♯, the fourth step in the downward motion from the start; the confusion lies in the status of the connecting G♯, which we must once again reinterpret, hearing it now as we suspected at first—as a passing tone to F♯ in the overall descent pattern. G♯ is still the wrong mode (and is further inappropriate in that, apart from the unique accent the composer places on it, it has received nowhere near the emphasized treatment that the other steps in the descent have), but it is the only way we seem to have here of getting from the A to the F♯. But notice, at least, that the very next notes, A–F♯, effect a clarification of just this unclear portion of the descent by outlining the interval passed through.

This A–F♯ figure (which seems to get repeated in more elaborate form in the next measure, with the B grace note adding to the A, and the downbeat G of measure 12 moving directly to F♯ followed by a skip) also resembles the earlier neighbor embellishments of notes established as "next in line." That is, here again a principal note is embellished, in a particular rhythmic pattern, with a higher note. But the interval of a minor third would seem to be a very unusual neighbor-type embellisher, and only when we bother to notice the slight change in the first two such embellishments does the pattern become clear. For such is the intervallic form of the minor scale that B, the fifth degree, is neighbored by C (forming a half step), while A, the fourth degree, is neighbored by B (forming a whole step). The next larger interval, of course, is three half steps, the minor third. So the A–F♯ alternation would seem to follow naturally in this progression of increasing neighbor distances (Ex. 4–4), even if we would not hear A as the neighbor of F♯ in any other context.

Ex. 4-4

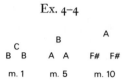

The downward motion would seem to stop here, for after the section break the line picks up again with B, its starting point. The overall progress, then, has been B–A–G♯–F♯, from the fifth degree down to the second. The interrupted journey seems to resemble other such downward attempts we have witnessed; it doesn't quite reach its goal, and must start again from the original point and rework its way to the tonic. The exact form of the end of the melody in this first section makes clear the progress to this point, for the special elaborated form of A–F♯ that leads into the wandering section-division segment (Ex. 4–5) actually summarizes the B to F♯ motion, this time properly supplying the G♮ (in place of the troublesome G♯ in the actual descent).

Ex. 4-5

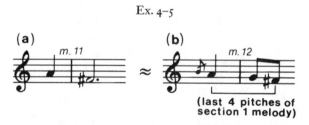

(last 4 pitches of section 1 melody)

The relation between (a) and (b) in Ex. 4–5 is illuminated in part by the melody in measure 9, where the clear a-minor context (as suggested by both tune and accompaniment) leaves no doubt that the on-the-beat D functions as an accented neighbor to the rhythmically weaker C. In measure 12, then, we can learn to regard the strong G as the neighbor to the weaker F♯, thus confirming A–F♯ as the essential motion (the B is purposely a grace note here, so the primacy of A is not in question). And then this form of rhythmic interpretation leads the way to understanding the melody in the connecting measure 12. As we discovered previously, the harmony at this point arrives at the B triad. Using this triad as reference, we can interpret the G and the C as neighbors (accented, incomplete) to the chordal F♯ and B respectively. The following three pitches outline the triad, and then the D♮, confusing the modes, reminds us of the G–G♯ modal confusion that just concerned us in the B–A–G–F♯ summary at the end of section 1, as well as in the A–F♯ summary of the earlier A–G♯–F♯ motion.

We know now what the melody of section 2 needs to do, and we even know that the melody resumes immediately with a repetition of the opening music, so our reorientation in the descent should be simple. We will not fully analyze the second half of the melody, but we can follow its essential course quite directly.

The melody of course picks up with B, neighbored again by C. In measure 16 the descent continues to an inappropriate A♯ (which, however, must remind us of the similarly placed and identically sounding B♭ of measure 4!), and then gets seriously sidetracked into configurations that clearly seem to recall the previous melodic interruptions (in measures 9 and 12). Each such flight from the straight path seems more elaborate than the previous, and this one seems to form a kind of climax. The end result, however, is the F♯ of measures 18–19–20 (like the resulting F♯ of measure 10), and this time the second degree clearly descends into the tonic. Appropriately, this tonic arrival is heralded by the useful anticipation figure (measures 20–21) we have seen before in this descent (measures 1 and 7). And when it is reached it is treated just like previous steps in the line, embellished by its upper neighbor in the usual pattern.

Finally, E receives its own special treatment at the end, apparently as a way of separating it from previous (less important) scale degrees that have otherwise received the same amount of elaboration and confirmation. This is the separated cadential slice that follows the unique silence in measure 23. (We will later see why, in terms of the harmony that accompanies this melodic unfolding, this cadence is even more necessary). The subject of the melody for this brief statement is E, which is supplied with its lower neighbor, D♯. This lower-neighbor shape forms a contrast with all the previous upper-neighbor forms, and directly balances the immediately previous E–F♯–E shape. But, over the course of the *entire* piece, it seems most fundamentally to form a balancing shape to the original B–C–B motion, which started the descent that ends here (Ex. 4–6). The connection of these two displays of triad pitches forms an elegant summary of the essential melodic motion over the span of the piece, and thus functions similarly to the distinct changes

Ex. 4–6

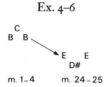

m. 1–4   m. 24–25

in pitch arrangement in the otherwise similar first and last chords
(see page 42).[4]

   We already know something about how this melody is accompanied.
The initial B is part of the tonic e triad, as is, of course, the final E; and
both these notes are appropriately accompanied. This produces the two-
dimensional (melodic and harmonic) e-minor "box" that frames the
piece. In the way that these first and last pitches are connected by the
intervening scalar steps, the first and last chords are connected by the
B[7] chord that concludes the first section. That B[7] chord coincides with
the arrival of F♯ in the scalar descent, and so the overall linear progress
to that point (B–F♯) describes an interval of the B triad, which is stated
at that point (Ex. 4–7).

Ex. 4–7

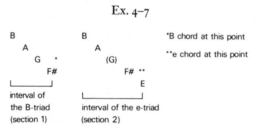

   The problem we face now is to interpret the less usual chords that
occur between these important signposts. First we must consider an important question: how seriously should we regard as an item for identification the sound resulting from the combination of a chord and its
simultaneous melody note? This was not an issue in the chordal piece
of the first chapter because all voices moved together, and the melody

4. At the same time, the cadential half-step neighbor form allows us to see a
contraction in the sizes of neighbor shapes that just balances the *expansion* we discovered earlier. For the half step, whole step, minor third series witnessed at the
start of the piece now appears in reverse: minor third (measure 19), whole step
(measure 21), half step (measure 24)!

did not seem to be a distinct and separate aspect of the music. But here, with the melody moving at one surface speed and the accompaniment proceeding at its own rate, we may be tempted to isolate, perhaps artificially, an eighth-note chord, even though the total sound at any one point would really be the resultant of *all* the intervals present (within the chord as well as between the chord and the melody). This is not a problem at the point of the first downbeat (or, for that matter, at any of the important harmonic-melodic stations), for here the melody note is just a duplication of a pitch contained in the accompanying chord.

A simple test case occurs in measure 1, at the point where the melody note changes: on beat four the total sound consists of C, E, G, and B. Do we wish to hear this as other than an e-minor chord? For example, if we insist on hearing chords in terms of some root established by stacking the notes in thirds, then we would have to hear this item as some kind of C chord. This is a typical pitfall of the habit of labelling items without regard to their context, and an understanding of the *functions* of the notes involved produces a much more fruitful result. Here, for example, the C functions, as we have discovered, as an ornament for the previous B: it is a temporary replacement of B. As such, it should not disturb in an identifying sense the chord continuing on underneath, which is still understood as an e-minor triad. This is not to say that we do not hear a dissonant sound at this point: to be sure, we hear an e-minor chord with an out-of-place melody note. But we have a way of understanding that melody note, of relating it to its neighboring melodic pitches, and (because we can relate those neighboring melodic pitches to the present chord that carries them) to the chord as well.

So when we arrive at the downbeat of the second measure and meet a chord that consists of the pitches F♯, A, and E, we can interpret that chord in isolation if it doesn't match its melody note in any familiar way. In this case neither the separable F♯–A–E nor the total F♯–A–E–B makes any direct triadic sense, and we shall have to examine the context in which these notes arise to arrive at an understanding of the chord. This approach is really no different from our consideration of the fourth-beat sound of measure 1.

In this case the notes A, F♯ seem to arise from the immediately preceding B, G of the e-minor chord, while the E is just a retained pitch. If we view the downbeat chord this way, with the F♯ and A as neighbors to (or passing tones from, depending on what happens next) notes of the previous chord, then we are actually viewing the chords as products of separate but coordinated *voices*. This is really the method developed in the first chapter, and will solve many problems in this more difficult context. The very form of the music as we already see it suggests such an approach, for if the B and G of the measure 1 chord generate a downward motion through the A and F♯ of measure 2, then these initial two notes correspond to the first *melodic* note, which of course also initiates a long downward motion.

Now if all three voices of the chords moved down by step together on the downbeat of measure 2, the result would be a simple V^7-type chord (F♯–A–D♯, with the E moving down to D♯; in fact, the addition of the melodic B at that point would complete a B^7 sonority). Since they do not, we can safely say that this downbeat chord needs no simple name to identify it, since we can otherwise understand all the notes that result in that chord. On the other hand, if we *expect* the E to follow suit and descend to D♯, then we can regard this chord as a *partial* B^7 formation (in its usual capacity as dominant embellisher of the e chord), with one pitch *not yet in place.*

Both interpretations come into play in measure 2; when we first hear the chord, we think of it in the first-mentioned way. But on beat 3 the E *does* descend (no matter what the spelling, the sonority on beat 3 is that of the B^7), and in retrospect we can hear the downbeat chord in the second-mentioned way.

At this point, however, matters get further complicated. When the melodic B is replaced by the neighbor C in measure 2, we are faced with a different situation from that in measure 1, where the C does not threaten the stability of the ongoing e-minor chord in the accompaniment. This new C, in replacing B, robs the B^7 sonority of its very root pitch, and changes the total sonority into a diminished-seventh chord (which again has no clear triadic identity). If only C will return to B in measure 3 (which is expected, on the order of the previous melodic formations), the dominant quality will be restored and the B^7 chord can perform its usual function by returning to the e chord from which it arose. But by the time C returns to B, the F♯ of the chord moves further down, to F♮, and the sonority is changed again.

Once again we have a chord that is no triad, but that arose from something we were ready to hear in triadic terms. This new chord, F–A–E♭, might sound like an F^7 chord, especially if the B moves once again to C. But by the time *that* happens, other voices making up this chord have continued *their* descent (as did the F♯ voice when it moved to F).

As we proceed through section 1 we see the three bass voices gradually descending from their starting points in the e-minor chord to their first resting place in the B⁷ chord of measure 12. The individual descents are unevenly paced, and it is this lack of coordination that produces the complex, rich and fascinating flux between clarity and ambiguity both in the chords and in their relation to the gradually descending melody they accompany. Every so often the alignment of these voices produces a familiar sonority: E⁷ on the downbeat of measure 4, D⁷ on the downbeat of measure 5, a minor and d minor in parts of measures 3, 9, 10, and 11. But the d-minor chord of measure 3 hardly seems worthy of the label, since it appears in a very confused context (and clashes with the B in the melody); and the dominant-seventh types may *suggest* their implied tonic references, but certainly do not behave like applied dominants, since they do not move on in the usual V–I fashion. In this sense these more familiar conjunctions of the bass lines seem almost like chance confluences of linearly significant elements; alternatively, we may find the suggestions offered by these familiar chords an enriching aspect of the overall movement from i to V⁷ over section 1. In any case it is worthwhile to examine each of these chords, familiar or not, in order to make the most of the music (as well as to gain experience in interpretation). To choose just one example, the area around measure 9 is interesting, since it forms a kind of oasis of triadic stability and recognizability. This is the region where the melody so clearly follows the a-minor triad as a referential structure, and we now find the harmony equally clear (with the second beat of measure 9 being actually the first consonant sound since the first chord of the piece!). The a-minor chord of measure 9 is led into by the strange downbeat chord of that measure; but this downbeat sonority is a link between the embellishing (dominant-type) diminished-seventh chord at the end of measure 8 and the a-minor arrival in measure 9. The B of the diminished seventh is retained into measure 9, while the other two voices, represented now by F and D, descend to E and C (thus arriving at the a triad before the B does). The chord on the downbeat is thus the result of these unaligned descents, just as is the chord on the downbeat of measure 2. In turn, of course, this very a-minor station is seen as an incomplete attempt at the ultimate B⁷ chord, which is then won by the descent of the E and C into D♯ and B (Ex. 4–8).

Ex. 4–8

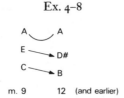

Before going on to observe some of the harmonic material in section 2, we can also note that these separable voices of the section one chords all descend to describe intervals of the three fundamental triads of the section: the top voice moves from E to A in clear, uninterrupted chromatic fashion, thus outlining an interval of the a triad, the only subject of stationary harmony in the section; the middle voice establishes a connection between B and D♯, presenting an interval of the V chord that concludes the section; and the lowest voice connects G with B, arpeggiating an interval of the i chord that initiates the section. In contrast we shall see that the lines of the section 2 accompaniment describe, over the course of the section, only intervals of the e-minor triad.

Naturally the harmony takes part in the repetition that begins the second section, so all bass voices are restored at that point to their original places in the e-minor triad. Once again, these voices begin their uncoordinated, descending chromatic journeys, producing along the way the same kinds of illusive and variably recognizable chords. But just as the melody becomes seriously sidetracked in this section (interrupting its descent with the climactic motion in measures 16–18), so does the chord-voice complex. The B octave in measure 17 is a striking event here, and is surely an important part of this climactic departure; as a representative of the dominant chord, this octave seems to serve as a link between the e chord that initiates section 2 and the final e chord of the piece.[5]

From this point on we can identify much of the harmony in conventional terms. For the B octave is followed by an embellishing diminished seventh that leads directly to the e triad at the end of measure 17 (with

5. It is interesting to link up this unique B octave with the treble C, the highest note of the piece. These two are joined in this moment of thickest texture, widest registral spread, and greatest dynamic force; they are the result of the preceding pressing stretto, and they are the boundaries of the only simultaneous three-register activity in the piece. This stridently dissonant pair recaptures the initial, linear B–C pair that originally establishes the whole mode of the actions of the piece. Note that the first B–C pair occurs in a register just central to the climactic spread these notes enclose here. (Note also the accented middle-C–B pair in measure 12.)

G and B of that chord arriving early, on beat 3). The following two measures alternate the i and iv chords because of the neighbor motions centering on the B (Ex. 4–9). But this skeletal e chord looks more like

Ex. 4–9

an incomplete B^7 chord when the E descends to D♯ in measure 20. This would seem to bring us as far, harmonically, as section 1 does altogether: from i to V^7, via iv (and this progress uses the same amount of melodic material, B descending as far as F♯, as was matched with this much harmony of the earlier section).

Both parts, melody and accompaniment, are ready to resolve together now, the melodic F♯ into E, and the harmonic B^7 into the e triad. It is interesting to follow the interruptions this conclusion features; for although the F♯ moves directly to E on the downbeat of measure 21, the B^7 chord moves not to e but to a C triad (the standard deceptive cadence, V^7–VI). This deception detracts seriously from the sense of melodic resolution and provides the necessary interest for the three measures of E–F♯ melodic alternation that are necessary to have the E station resemble the prior important melodic stations. Instead of accompanying this E prolongation with a steady e triad, the composer uses this time to *fix into e* the straying harmony.

The E in measure 22 receives better accompaniment, with the (gradually accruing) E-major $^6_4$ chord. Things look better still with the e-minor chord that ends the measure; but of course this is not permanently sufficient, since it is still not the best inversion (the weak inversion of the first chord of the piece would hardly be rectified by this resolution). And then, just as we seek a root-position e triad, we hear instead a chord very far from that indeed: the German sixth chord on the downbeat of measure 23 is a shocking departure from the expected, and can best be understood in terms of linear motion—the E of the melody and the G of the upper bass voice have arrived in place (in the e triad), while the bottom B has split into its two neighbors, C and B♭ (A♯ would obviously be a better spelling). Of course, after the pregnant silence the neighbors contract back to the basic B, and all that is needed is to change the $^6_4$ inversion into the root position chord.[6]

This is just the function of the separated cadence here. The bass B restores the nonchord tones into B, and the first chord appears as a combination of i and V (B, F♯ of V; B, E of i). It is impossible to say whether this downbeat chord is a i$^6_4$ with an "early" F♯ or a V with E momentarily replacing (and then directly moving to) D♯: these two constructs are really indistinguishable. And by combining characteristics of both chords, this downbeat chord is all the richer in meaning for this piece: by partaking of the i chord, the chord contributes to a i–V–i statement in the cadence, thereby summarizing the fundamental harmonic slicing of the piece (i, measure 1; V, measure 12; i, last measure); and by partaking of the V chord, the downbeat chord directly picks up from the (unresolved) V^7 of the preceding passage, and resolves it directly in a clear, unambiguous V–i statement (the only such entirely unencumbered statement of the entire composition).[7] When we recall now that this separated cadence also serves a summarizing *melodic* function (the E neighbor expression, balancing the original B neighbor expression), we grasp the full import of the total separation of this figure from the main body of the piece.

Even with portions of the music left relatively unanalyzed, this composition now appears to exhibit all the kinds of coherence we have been discovering in simpler pieces. Goal-directed motion was seen to take place over the span of the piece, and within a two-dimensional matrix of unified, tonic-triad, common reference. The liberal use of standard labels is considerably less threatening to understanding and discovery now and can serve wherever needed as a useful shorthand for the basic coherence it should be meant to imply. We are thus prepared to range over the tonal literature in search of a wealth of tonal invention.

6. Though we have abandoned the longer-range bass lines, we can see how this resolution creates e-minor-triad end points for these lines; since triad notes also initiated the lines in section 2, all lines describe triad intervals. This is a rectification of the overall linear condition of section 1.

7. Additionally, by combining E and F♯ in the same chord (the only notes besides the unambiguous B, the ones we must choose between if we want a single-root interpretation) a reference is made to the previous linear *alternation* of these two pitches in the last portion of the melody. Compare the discussion of the verticalized B–C pair of measure 17.

Analysis of Bach: Two-Part Invention in d minor

With some relief, no doubt, we step back to a simpler texture with this two-voice composition. On the other hand, with more experience behind us (and especially with some success in a case of greater surface complexity), we should be prepared for more intense scrutiny of these lines and the harmonies they jointly imply. As before, we shall divide our attention between overall formal accomplishment and the details of local continuity. Portions of the music left unanalyzed this time will include not those that overreach our present scope, as in the previous study, but rather those that can be studied just in terms of other passages covered in the text.

Once again any edition of this readily available piece will serve. But it should be understood that Bach's compositions were originally notated without dynamic or articulative performance directions. And so any such directions appearing in an edition only represent an editor's ideas, and are not to be taken seriously as the composer's intentions. Our attention should be focused on a pitch solely because something about the rhythm or the pitch environment highlights that pitch; we need not draw a relation between two accented pitches or two very loud pitches, since these attributes of the notes were not determined by the composer.

An immediate problem, of a sort not encountered previously, engages us as we begin to search for an overall orientation of the music: no obvious sectional punctuations or textural changes appear to suggest a carving of the music into fundamental units of progression. Without such a comprehensive view of the surface, we might have to observe the detailed unfolding of the music measure by measure, constantly bearing in mind the progress to date, constantly groping for a sense of movement on a larger scale.

But fortunately the piece only appears to have an undifferentiated surface if we insist on finding obvious points of reference, such as total silences or total repetitions. If we become attuned to the kind of activity that makes up the surface of this piece, we soon discover points of subtle departure from that activity.

For example, notice that, in general, the music features an attack on every sixteenth-note position of every measure (in one voice or the other, and often in both at the same time). In this sense the trill starting in measure 19 seems not so much a special event as just an intensification of an obvious quality of the music. But in measure 17 we have for the first time a sixteenth-note position that is not attacked in either voice: that is, toward the end of measure 17 both voices are slackening their pace *at the same time*. As we study this event we soon find that other kinds of unique "slackenings" appear in conjunction with this rhythmic gap. The treble voice of measure 17 presents the first linear unison of the piece; this is a slackening of the intervallic pace of the music, which up to this point has featured a pitch change at every new attack. This unison is followed directly by two other such unchanging figures (F and C). Finally, the downbeat of measure 18 presents the first vertical "unison" (in the obvious sense that an octave is a pitch-class "unison") of the piece, which represents a slackening of the vertical (harmonic) inter-vallic tension. Especially since the vertical F octave is coupled with the linear F-anticipation figure and is placed on a downbeat, we can, in the light of all these subtle surface changes, make a slice at this point; we then consider the minute surface details surrounding this point (the downbeat of measure 18) as signals of the arrival of a section ending (and the consequent beginning of a new section).

Once we are attuned to the kinds of events that can be understood as changes in the surface activity, we can more easily recognize the same combination of departing features in measures 36–38. In the first two of these measures there are again some unattacked sixteenth-note positions in both voices simultaneously, *and these are the first recurrences* of this change since measure 17. The repeated A over the measure 37–38 bar line and the octave A on the downbeat of measure 38 are the next appearances of *these* devices after the first slice point. So we can think of the music from measure 18 up to the downbeat of measure 38 as a second section of the piece.

After a total absence of these devices—either singly or in combination—they appear twice again in combination: in measures 48–49 and, shortly thereafter, at the end of the piece. But measures 48–49 lack one important feature, the downbeat octave (which is here replaced by the thoroughly ordinary major third). Since a complete combination of elements comes so soon after to "correct" this deviation, we need not slice additionally at this point, but can think of the rest of the music, from measure 38 to the end of the piece, as the third and final section. Since the last, full combination of devices is also the last event of the piece, our sense of the earlier combinations as *section endings* is powerfully reinforced.

Now although it may not be very interesting to note that this piece is obviously in d minor (since every tonal piece is in a key, and sets about exploring the resources of its own home-base triad), it is surely interesting to note one *way* that this piece exhibits the d-minor triad: the succession of these unique octaves exactly describes the triad—F, A, D. The notes of the tonic triad, then, carve the music into its sections. And as we become familiar with the contents of these sections, we will see that each section has as its local tonic the pitch class featured at the slice point that begins that section. Section one begins in the home-base d minor and gradually changes the focus of reference to F. Section two begins in F and delivers the music into the control of A. The final section begins in a minor and restores the local reference to d minor by the end of the piece; but since d minor is then the first and last reference triad (like the first and last chords of the piece of the first chapter), and since the d-minor triad provides the pitches for the intermediary tonicizations, we see how the d-minor triad actually *controls the pitch activity of the entire composition.*

An understanding of how these key changes take place will not only enrich our overall view of the piece, but will also provide an entry into the world of detail at the level of surface continuity.

That the music opens "in d minor," of course, just means that the notes in circulation are those of the d-minor collection,[1] that among those notes the pitches of the d-minor triad are referential, and that the pitch class D is acting as home base. If the music changes focus to F, then we must see all of these constructs switched (to the F collection, the F triad and F itself as tonic). When we later study the opening melody we will pin down some ways that it displays the d-minor triad; at the moment, however, we can note that the first simultaneities of the piece present the intervals of the d-minor triad (Ex. 5–1) just at the same time that the

Ex. 5–1

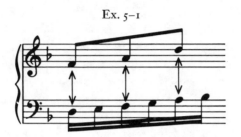

upper line outlines that triad in the most straightforward manner. For the first seven measures the first measure of each pair clearly outlines this triad both linearly and vertically (harmonically). And the measures between these d-minor presentations describe, both linearly and harmonically, a neighbor collection to the d-minor triad. (This collection, C♯, E, G, and B♭, consists of the remaining notes of the scale and forms a chord of the dominant type—the embellishing diminished seventh).

So the d-minor scale provides all the notes for the opening music. As for the use of D as tonic, we can point to the downbeats every two measures (measures 1, 3 in the bass, 5 in the treble, etc.), as well as the unique linear octave in the bass part of measure 7.

The scale, triad, and tonic focus of d minor, as exhibited by the opening music, are gradually shifted to those of F major, with the shift completed, of course, at the downbeat vertical octave F in measure 18, the

1. We need not delve into the fictitious question of "what kind of minor" we are dealing with. The "natural" minor *collection*, which is equivalent to the major collection (the two scales just start in different places), is the basic construct. The seventh degree gets raised whenever it is acting as a leading tone; then the sixth degree also gets raised *if* it is acting in conjunction with the raised seventh (as when six is moving through seven on the way to eight). The styles of minor can be thought of as one collection with changeable sixth and seventh steps.

point where section 2 begins "in F." This octave declares F as tonic (and would seem to function as an equivalent to the lone D downbeat in measure 1). The change of scale contents should be very easy since the natural d-minor collection is exactly that of F, note for note. If only the pitch class D stops being a focus, then the sixth and seventh degrees of the d-minor scale will no longer be raised. In their normal (lowered) forms, they will join with the other notes of the d-minor collection to present, just as well, the F collection. This is what happens starting in measure 7, after which point the notes are drawn from what is clearly the common F–d scale contents.

As for the change in triad the V(-type)–i alternations for the d triad shown in the first few measures give way to appearances of V–I pairs for F: measures 9–10 present the first such pair, followed by others in 12–13 (the V chord itself sometimes being substituted for by other V-type configurations, like the neighboring E–G–Bb–D structure that surrounds the F triad) and 15–16–17–18.

More hidden details of the music further point to the establishment of F (and its scale and triad) as the new home base. For example, the upper voice comes to its first temporary halt in measure 12; the stopping note is G. Another brief halt occurs two measures later, with the note F. Both these points are introduced by sequenced figures (Ex. 5–2),

Ex. 5–2

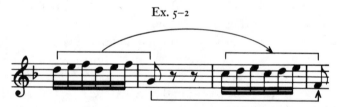

and all these factors combine to produce a strong sense of arrival at the pitch F via a second-degree–first-degree resolution. In fact, through the use of sequence, an entire descending F scale, starting just at the point where the collection of notes can be interpreted in either d or F, and ending just with the definitive F octave at the section division, is presented to us. The downbeat F of measure 7 initiates a two-measure sequence that descends to E on the downbeat of 9. The downbeat two measures later picks up with D, which likewise initiates a sequence (the same one that pushes G–F our way, via its end points) that descends to C two measures later. So the downbeats every two measures starting with measure 7 describe the upper portion of the F scale, and these points, because they are projected by sequences, strongly condition the shapes of notes surrounding them. After the completion of the sequence unit that brought the scale to C, the next note is Bb: it is a beat early if we continue to expect these points every second downbeat. This premature arrival surely hastens the descent, and in fact the very next two notes are A and G (significantly they are eighth notes, slow enough in themselves to be taken seriously as points in this line of emphasized steps), which nearly complete the scale. An interrupting summary actually completes the scale (even overshoots it) in a weak way, but the second degree powerfully reappears in the measure 17 anticipation figure and moves forcefully and definitively down to F with the next anticipation figure, which ends in the all-important F octave (these scale-concluding items are, of course, just the unique events we noticed at first, leading us to slice the music at this point).

In similar fashion we can trace the way section 2 brings the focus of tonality from F to A, and how the final section restores the original d triad as local (and, in sum, overall) source of reference. In so doing, we will have covered most of the harmonic activity of the music. In section 1, for example, only a few chordal usages do not play directly into the original V–i proclamation of d minor or the gradual replacement of that triad by the F triad. These other chords, however, can easily be seen to relate to chords that are principal factors in the general harmonic progression. The first such chord, for example, is the g-minor array of measure 8, which clearly functions as a link between the d-minor triad of measure 7 and the C (= V of F, and so used here) display of measure 9. In other words, at this point d and F are directly connected in the cycle of fifths.

Section 2 begins with a solid expression of the F tonality, alternating the F triad with dominant-type neighbor collections to that triad. The appearance of the D^7 chord in measure 23 is not surprising when we realize that the interval A–C is shared by this chord and the F triad (notice how the expression of the F triad in the previous measure displays this interval prominently in the bass), and that this D^7 chord initiates a cycle-of-fifths connection back to the F triad from which it arose (with the D^7 as dominant to g minor in measure 24, which then leads through the C of measure 25 into F in 26; the entire parenthesized motion from a chord of D to F seems to recapitulate the harmonic progress of the

piece thus far). So F is the certain harmonic basis of the section to this
point; but the next measure introduces a foreign element—the E chord,
which apparently serves as dominant to the a-minor triad of measure 28.
The extensive E-prolongation represented by the trill is the principal
long-range motivation for the arrival of a minor in measure 38. This
trill obviously picks up on the function of the previous trill on C, which
is a dominant expression of the newly established F tonality just as the
E trill is a dominant *preparation* for the future a tonality. The high A
in measure 36; the iv–V–i outline from 36 to 38, matched with a rhythmic
compression (the weakness of the downbeat of measure 37 suggests a
hearing of the six beats of measures 36–37 as three groups of two beats
each) that seems to hurry the arrival of the a cadence; and the clear
second-degree–first-degree linear motion into the cadence in measures
37–38 all contribute to the definitive point of modulation at the section
division. Such a brief tracing of the harmonic workings of this section
can serve as a framework for closer textual study, leading to further
discovery of the use of detail in the composition.

   Once a is established it is not subjected to the same stable treatment
that characterized the d and F regions. For example, the a scale is not
even present after the point of arrival. No sooner does a arrive than it
seems just a dominant for d. This motion itself could accomplish the
move back to the original triad; but a more gradual approach is taken,
with the D forming a link in a dominant chain that leads to F on the
downbeat of measure 42. Immediately this F is reinterpreted as the third
of the d-minor triad, and from that point on the harmony reads out
clearly in d minor. This swift transition from F into d depends on the
shared interval A–F, which is struck in the treble voice and presented,
with a passing tone, in the bass voice at the same time. It is not until the
end of measure 42 that we must reinterpret the A–F interval as one of
the d-minor triad.

   The deceptive cadence on the downbeat of measure 49 forms the only
wrinkle in the otherwise clear d-minor music of the last 11 measures.
This V–VI motion is embodied in the deliberately misleading use of the
special surface combination that otherwise has been reserved for section
divisions, and so here powerfully suggests that the A^7 chord of measure
47 will resolve to d, bringing the music to rest. Its failure to do so requires
that the cadence be reworked, as it is in the last measures.

   It may seem peculiar to spend so much time studying the harmonic aspects of a composition whose surface is just two lines. But, as the bass part of the Chopin composition should suggest, the surface, "stylistic" emphasis on one dimension does not alter the basic two-dimensional quality of the music. It should be clear, moreover, that in this present composition when we refer to a "chord" we are just as well talking about combinations of intervals spanned (and filled in) by the lines as we are about the vertical alignment of notes. Our study of the "harmonic" progress of the piece, then, has not at all been restricted to vertical considerations, and many strictly linear details were interpreted in terms of their contribution to this picture. Further study of the lines in this way is recommended, and, for a typical case, we can examine the linear aspects of the deceptive cadence just discussed.

The representatives of the V chord in measure 48 are, at the point of resolution, C♯ (treble) and A (bass). If C♯ moves to D (thus completing a linear move into the triad) and A moves to D (thus arpeggiating an interval of the d triad), the d triad will be represented, and will resolve the V chord. The C♯ does move to D, but the A moves to its upper neighbor, B♭. It is this B♭ that forces us to reinterpret the D as the third of a VI chord, the B♭ triad. The B♭ does not immediately return to A, but seems to move to G, the next downbeat, which is the *lower* neighbor to A. The resolution of the neighbor group is the penultimate bass pitch, A, which then moves directly to the long-expected and missed D (Ex. 5–3). The deceptive cadence at measure 49 can be seen as the product

Ex. 5–3

(treble line)	C#	D	....		
(bass line)	A	B♭	G	A	D
m.	48	49	50	51	52

of a misalignment of linear speeds. The treble C♯ moves immediately into its goal, D; but the matching bass A just prolongs itself for several measures, only switching to D at the end.

As the essential triadicity of the music (how it expresses its tonic triad both for the entire piece and in the local detail) becomes clear, we can safely turn our attention to some interesting aspects of the lines. After all, we have not even examined the opening motive, which, through various imitative means, seems to generate the entire fabric of the invention. Feeling secure in our knowledge that the lines are embedded in a successful and coherent grammatical environment, we can proceed to regard the surface activity of the music as the unique and special formation that it is. One more analogy to human language may be appropriate here: once we gained experience in translating German poems (that is, dealing with them primarily as instances of the German language) we would profit greatly by starting to view the poems as individual *poetic* statements (which could scarcely be done before we understood the "German" of them).

The very way that the opening motive displays the triad is unusual: the span of the ascending line is D–Bb (which overshoots, and thus hides, the defining D–A interval). Of course, the placement of the d-triad notes on the three beats already sufficiently differentiates among the six notes, so we can view the E and the G as passing tones. But the function of the Bb is unclear until the motive reverses itself in the second measure, and the Bb, still on a weak portion of a beat, returns to the A, which is again on the beat. With regard to shape, then, the two-measure motive is clearly generated out of its own first measure, and this continuation seems necessary in terms of the unresolved Bb at the end of the first part of the motive.

But two aspects of the motive are still unclear: the appearance of the C♯, which splits the two halves of the form, and the lack of completion (back to D) at the end of the motive. The two problems are really linked, since we can view the C♯ in parallel with the Bb—as a neighbor to the opposite triad note. But this neighbor shape is not completed locally, since no D returns in this middle register to reclaim the C♯ (Ex. 5–4). The lack

Ex. 5–4

The motive is generated from this background by arpeggiating the vertical intervals and filling some of them in with scalar passing tones.

of this completion, then, motivates the entire composition to continue, just as the failure of the Bb to resolve immediately motivates the reversal-completion of the motive. It is interesting to note that the *very* last pitch of this upper voice is the missing middle D.

The direct imitation of the motive that first appears in the bass part is just the most obvious way that the shape of the motive conditions later form in the piece. Much more interesting, because of its subtlety, is the form of the first accompanying figure. The arpeggiation of the d-minor triad in the treble part of measure 3 would seem to be just a convenient and standard accompaniment to the statement of the motive in the other part. But first of all, this particular shape directly clarifies the hidden triadic structure of the first measure (by isolating the triad notes and eliminating the passing tones); second, the shape of the accompaniment is just that of the motive—an ascent spanning a sixth.

Because the second measure of accompaniment merely repeats this shape (in fact, simply seems to flesh out the d-minor skeleton with scalar filler!), and because the bass part continues its literal imitation, and finally because the treble part then picks up with an octave-higher repeat of the opening music, we can account for all shapes in the first six or seven measures in terms of the very first measure. In fact, if we think of the motive as an ascent through a sixth followed by a large skip in the opposite direction, we can see how the accompaniment even picks up on this continuation, since the rising d triad in measure 3 is followed by a balancing skip down to the G (which initiates the next rising-sixth shape).

The sequence starting in measure 7 introduces some new music, but with really very little trouble (just thinking of the original motive in new ways) we can relate the new shapes to the old. The second measure of the sequenced unit (measure 8) of course resembles the second half of the motive. The first measure of the sequence can be thought of in terms of the first measure of the motive since the rising scale is followed by a large skip in the opposite direction; the scale does not rise as far (spanning a fifth rather than a sixth) because it starts one attack late, a minor third having been added before it. But this affixing of the minor third, in the opposite direction to the scalar climb, derives from the motive, which *follows* its scalar climb with an interval in the opposite direction (and this interval is even a minor-third type, spelling notwithstanding). Furthermore, if we read the pitches starting with the scalar climb in measure 7 and including the Bb on the downbeat of measure 8, we find the same sequence of pitch classes (D–E–F–G–A–Bb) as was used for the first measure of the piece, here reshaped.

A second sequence follows this one, the unit of which is the treble figure in measures 11–12. This unit also derives from the original motive shape, for the rising six-note scale is here represented by two adjacent three-note scales, as if the original shape had been pressed into a smaller space (Ex. 5–5). The relationship is even closer than the shape alone

Ex. 5–5

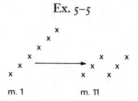

would suggest, since the three-note unit is just d–e–f, the first three notes of the original scale form. And this d–e–f is registered one octave higher than the original, a position presaged by the repeat of the original motive an octave higher in measure 5. Finally, notice that the sequence unit ends with the skip in the opposite direction—a further connection to the generator of all these shapes (Ex. 5–6). It is interesting to note that this d–e–f version of the motive occurs just where we are beginning to notice a d to f switch in tonality.

Ex. 5–6

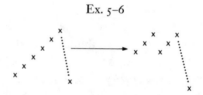

The new three-note shape, as derived from the six-note shape, ac-counts for most of the remaining music up to the end of the first section. The bass line in measures 8 and 10 follows this form, as does the treble in measures 14–15. The two bass examples actually display the connection between the three-note line and the six, since three notes in a row are isolated *metrically*, but actually extend forward from a *prior* step. This would seem to negate the motive, until we notice that, around the octave interruption, the entire two-measure unit actually climbs a sixth (Ex. 5–7).

With the exception of an octave or two, the entire first section of the piece reads out in terms of the opening motive. Significantly, it is just at the F cadence, the section division, that the music seems *not* to

Ex. 5–7

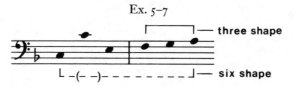

The entire unit is sequenced, calling attention to its form.

relate in this way: measure 17, calling our attention to the end of a section, presents shapes that depart from the going activity. (It is just here that we first noticed some peculiarities in the surface, leading us to our initial, and fruitful, slicing).

Significantly, as we begin to hear section 2 we encounter a new element, the ascending fifth in the treble leading to the new trill (for which the repeated C's may be a preparation). Of course, these new elements, signs of a new section, just accompany imitations of the original music. Without doubt, these shapes pervade the entire fabric of the piece, and further study is recommended to uncover instances of this kind of coherence on many levels. For example, it is very interesting to hear a gradually rising six-note line, an embedded augmentation of the opening measure shape, described by the treble downbeats starting in measure 30, and leading the way to the a-minor cadence. This rising line exactly spans middle C through the A above it, presenting an interval of the a-minor triad about to be tonicized.

To conclude, we might do well to review the course of this analytic study. Once again, a basic carving of the music resulted from simple observations about the general surface condition; this carving led the way to an overall harmonic understanding, which then served as a basis for understanding harmony locally. Linear motion was then seen to be an inseparable token of this harmonic progress, and at the same time linear coherence was studied with a greater intensity. This last aspect of the work sparked a new interest in the "pretriadic" features, with shape-related observations now resting on the secure tonal context we already established for this composition. Concurrently, then, we are continuing to discover how pieces are *tonal* pieces, and how they are tonal *pieces*.

Analysis of a
Schubert Song

Our subject for this study, a brief song composed by Schubert in 1815 and titled "Heidenröslein" (Ex. 6–1), presents a surface of utmost simplicity and clarity. With a melody obviously plainer than the lines of the Bach invention, harmonized in a manner that, compared with the Chopin prelude, must seem straightforward, this miniature provides a fine opportunity to assess our abilities for thorough analytic work. In such a concise musical statement every event can be thoughtfully considered; and, under the general influence of the G-major tonic triad, these considerations can flow abundantly from the two kinds of observations (those theoretically induced from the structure of the triad, and those stemming from unbiased perceptual study of the surface relations) now at our disposal.

A rich variety of relations, both of similarity and of subtle differentiation, among the surface formations immediately suggests a number of slicings concurrently. It doesn't seem to matter which path we first choose to follow, since all these surface elements seem to contribute to a unified sense of motion. For example, we can start by noticing that the last two measures separate themselves as a unit because the voice part is silent. (At the same time the piano departs from its previous

Ex. 6-1

accompaniment-type format to assume the more active and melodic style of the now absent voice.) This observation of differentiation links up with one of identity: the solo piano music in this final two-measure unit generally reproduces the voice-line music of the previous two measures. So we must regard measures 13–14 as a two-measure unit also, and a sense of progression by two-measure units now extends back four measures into the piece. Each of these units, then, functions as an ending—measures 13–14 for the voice line, measures 15–16 identically for the entire composition.

At the same time the fermata at the end of measure 12 makes a slice in the music at that point, and forcefully separates the final four measures as a unit. So we think of the two endings as making up a larger, general ending-unit.[1] (Of course the sense of metrical regularity splits each two-measure unit into single measures, so the general sense of successive layers of building blocks is very clear, at least at the end of the piece.)

One other fermata occurs, and this slice comes just two measures before the second fermata. So measures 11–12, bounded by gross stopping points, appear as yet another two-measure unit, extending the sense of even-sized units back further into the body of the music.

This combination of the most striking surface relations presents the music in two large areas: the first ten measures (as yet undifferentiated), and the last six (sliced into two plus two plus two). Two questions seem pertinent here, then. Since the second (six-measure) region is so obviously carved into units of two measures each, is there some subtler way that the two-measure unit constitutes a mode of motion through the first region? And is there any overall triadic accomplishment that aligns with (is projected by) this fundamental two-section progression?

Attacking the first question first (since it will not get us deeply involved in all aspects of the piece, as will the second question), we find that the voice part itself clearly moves through the first ten measures in two-measure spurts: the quarter note at the end of the second measure is the first such long note, and is followed again by faster motion; the rest at the end of measure 4 delineates another two-measure group (and, since the rest is a more definitive break than the quarter note, we tend to think of the first two two-measure groups as joined in a four-measure group, balancing the four-measure group at the end). Since measures 6 and 8 similarly end with pause effects in the voice, we see an even slicing of the entire first (ten-measure) region into these two-measure units (whose size is so clearly delineated in the last, six-measure, region).

Subtler distinctions in the piano part align with this subslicing. The first two measures, for example, present a constant bass G, which moves on with the downbeat of the third measure. After two measures of moving bass activity, another two static measures of G appear. So the first six measures are grouped by the piano music in just the way described by the voice line. Finally, the piano music of measures 7–8 is exactly duplicated in measures 9–10 (with the very important exception of one bass

1. Here the composer's special notice, "wie oben" (figuratively, "into the bargain"), is helpful; it may indicate that we are to perform the last four bars as a unit functioning in a summarizing or cadential manner.

pitch). And the identification of these last two-measure units completes
the piano contribution to the two-measure level of groupings. A picture
of the piece according to these slicings appears in Ex. 6–2 and portrays

Ex. 6–2

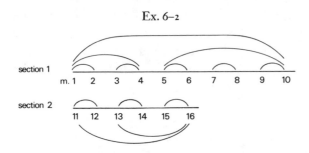

the sense of units at all levels. The one- and two-measure divisions combine to form the larger groupings, which, we shall see, each accomplish
a specific triadic task in a unified and directed piece-long motion.

Our second question, about the general functions of the two large
regions, we will answer only gradually, as it will entail study of many
deeper and more ongoing aspects of the piece. We can begin by studying
just the first four-bar phrase of the first section. This phrase separates
itself most strikingly, for the unique rest in the voice part and the return
of the constant bass G in the piano part are just two tokens of a fundamental large-scale articulation at measure 5: a new beginning, picking
up with the music first heard in measure 1. This first phrase accomplishes
a simple goal, an exposition of the home-base G-major triad.

Let us first notice how the G-major triad itself forms the boundary
material for the four-bar phrase. Measures 1 and 4 in the piano part
display only this triad, and the two intervening measures do not include
this chord. Furthermore, the first and last chords of the phrase (both G
major) are in root position, while none of the intervening chords are
so firm. A sense of moving away from and back to strong home-base
chords, by way of weaker intermediary chords, is thus established over
the first phrase.

At the same time the voice part follows the same pattern. The first
interval, B–D, is of the G-major triad. In measures 2 and 3, however, the
line seems not to describe an interval of the G chord, but rather one of
the D chord (D–A). Then in measure 4 the interval D–G refers to the
G triad once again, completing the motion.

The chords that connect the initial and final G expressions form a strong link between them. The A-based stack of measure 2 seems to be a small jump away from home base (all notes being just a step away, with the G remaining constant, as if to control the deviation); this chord moves through a chord of D back to the G chord, thus moving by dominants through the cycle of fifths.

But *linearly* the accompaniment is an even tighter expression of G. For the neighbors to the G chord that go to form the chord of measure 2 return to their original posts in measure 4, and they move back there by direct, but uncoordinated, means (Ex. 6–3). The easiest line to follow

Ex. 6–3

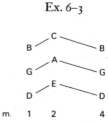

is the D line, which, after moving to E in measure 2, moves directly back to D in measure 3 (Ex. 6–4). The line emanating from the first D, then,

Ex. 6–4

```
      E
   D /   \ D — D
m.   1   2   3   4
```

is just a prolongation, via neighbor formation, of that G-triad note.

The middle line, starting on G, does not return directly to G after the neighbor motion in measure 2, but first dips down to the lower, balancing neighbor note, F♯ (Ex. 6–5). This line, then, likewise expresses a note of the tonic triad.

The upper line, beginning with B, is the least direct, but really adds only one complicating element to these paths. The B makes the basic

Ex. 6–5

```
       A — A
   G <          > G
       ____ F#
m.   1   2   3   4
```

neighbor move to C, and then, like the G line, dips down to the lower neighbor tone; but then, just before resolving both C and A to the generating B, the line inserts the pitch D, a "triad reference" pitch that interrupts the neighbor motion (Ex. 6–6). So this line, too, expresses its

Ex. 6–6

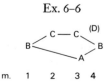

own first note. Additionally, with the D a step up from the C, we can see the G-triad interval B–D, complete with scalar passing tone, described by the line in a concurrent, subsidiary motion (Ex. 6–7).

Ex. 6–7

The bass line, of course, is also a product of the first G chord, and in the most interesting manner. In fact, the bass G generates a neighbor motion, in imitation of the upper three lines, and this motion is completely out of synchronization with the other neighbors. For the G moves to the neighboring F♯ *after* the other three lines move in initial coordination; and the F♯ does not return to G when the other three neighboring pitches resolve into the triad. In fact, the F♯ doesn't resolve within the phrase at all: it returns to a proper (that is, adjacently registered) G just on the first attack of the second phrase, at the downbeat of measure 5. The lack of resolution of the F♯, then, is a prime motivating factor for the continuation of the music past the otherwise satisfactory fourth measure (with so many other issues seeming to be resolved by the end of the first phrase) (Ex. 6–8).

Ex. 6–8

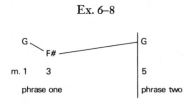

The interruption in this long-range neighbor motion is easy to interpret in terms of the G triad. The C is an incomplete upper neighbor to the B, and the G is simply a triad tone. (The two incomplete neighbors[2]—F♯ and C—of course form an interval of the intermediary D[7] chord and function in two dimensions at once, as pitches in the tonal system do.)

All these uncoordinated neighbor motions, expressing notes of the G-major triad, are aligned to form the *chords* that vertically prolong the G triad (by the motion described previously). Thus the four-bar phrase presents an exposition of the home-base triad in the typical two-dimensional matrix-type format. The locally unresolved F♯ in the bass line links the otherwise complete phrase to the rest of the composition. Just as the first phrase grows out of the G-major triad expressed by the first measure, the entire piece grows out of the G-major triad expressed by the first phrase. Note that the first measure is one-fourth of the first phrase, and the first phrase is just one-fourth of the composition.

We can now proceed to discover what the remainder of section 1 does with this well-established tonic triad. The first four-bar phrase is followed by a six-bar phrase that completes the first section. Whereas the first phrase is bounded by two G chords, the second starts with a G chord and moves to a D chord. Like the boundary chords of the first phrase, these new boundary chords are strong, root-position formations, and seem to be linked by one other root-position chord, that of b in measure 8. The succession of root-position triads, then, just spells out the home-base triad, G–B–D. We will now see how, after phrase 1 establishes the G-major triad as home base, the second phrase moves from that triad to the dominant triad, D. The entire focus of reference (tonic, triad, and scale collection) is changed over the course of this second phrase. Thus the entire shape of section 1 is clear.

First we can notice the change in the pitch contents. The difference between the G and D collections, of course, is just the difference of C and C♯. No C♯'s occur in the first phrase, and no C's in the second. Perhaps the change can be seen most succinctly in measure 6. Here we see

---

2. We must distinguish between incomplete neighbors "on the left side" and "on the right." Those that appear spontaneously (not generated out of the triad) but resolve *into* the triad note (like the bass C of measure 3) raise no issues. But those that come out of the triad and do not immediately return (like the bass F♯) create a sense of tension with their temporary nonresolution.

a slight departure in the otherwise straight repetition of the first two measures: the C's of measure 2 have become the C♯'s of measure 6. The effect here is clear: in measure 2 the D to A linear interval in the voice is filled in with scale tones of G; in measure 6, it is filled in with scale tones of D. In the earlier case an interval of one chord is arpeggiated and filled in with tones from the scale of another chord (G); but in the second, reworked case the interval and the scalar materials match. Another product of the change is that we can take the A^7 chord seriously as a dominant of D. (In measure 2, the a^7 chord, lacking the half-step leading tone to D, cannot be so considered.) Both these results point to a takeover by D of the local function of tonic.

But if measures 6–7 present a V^7–I motion in D, the sense of arrival is not very strong, for the D chord is not in root position. Therefore another A^7 chord appears, in measure 8, to try to rework the cadential effect. This time the action is even more unexpected, since the V chord moves to vi, with the standard deceptive cadence form. This arrival at b is most interesting, and forms the major link between the former and new tonalities, as observed before. Because it happens at the end of four measures, we see why the original four bars of the first phrase have to be expanded to six in the second phrase: the extension occurs at the point where A^7 could have moved to D, completing the phrase, but moves elsewhere instead. The motion through b, on the way to D, also accounts for the only pitch, A♯ in measure 9, that is foreign to the G/D collection set. For the vocal line in measures 7–8 can be read out in terms of the b-minor triad as well as the assumed D triad (since F♯–D is an interval shared by both these triads, and the scales, in the region where this interval is embedded, are identical). Then the voice figure in measure 9 exactly describes b minor (Ex. 6–9), with the otherwise mysterious A♯

Ex. 6–9

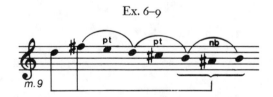

functioning as the leading tone to B in the lower-neighbor formation. This is not to say, of course, that the tonic focus is B: on the contrary, B is just a passing reference between the tonic poles of G and D. As

such, it is only obliquely stated. For example, this b-minor vocal statement is not even accompanied by b-minor harmonic materials. And the
one b triad, even if it is in root position, is not preceded by its own
dominant. Purposely, the emphasis is taken *off* B. But the inclusion of
hints of that tonality completes an elegant picture of the passage from
G to D by way of the appropriate, remaining G-triad member, B.

Next the extension of four measures into six provides time for a
final reworking of the cadence, with the A⁷ chord on the downbeat of
measure 10 moving directly to a firm D triad. Now that we have the
D triad as reference, we can go back and read some of the lines in the
previous measures in terms of the D triad. For example, the bass line from
measure 7 to the end of the section can be interpreted as in Ex. 6–10.

Ex. 6–10

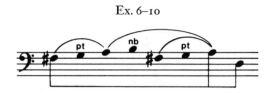

If we first think of the F♯ of measure 7 as just a neighbor to the more
fundamental bass G of measures 5–6 (in parallel to the obvious interpretation in the first three measures), we can now reinterpret the G as
a long, incomplete upper neighbor to the F♯, which now takes on triadic
significance in measure 7 (where, incidentally, it is now accompanied
by the new tonic chord; compare this with the harmonic situation in
measure 3).

Quite simply, section 2 (the final six measures of the song) just returns the tonic focus to G. Actually, this is accompanied in the two-
measure space between the two fermatas: the C♯ is now C again, so the
scale contents are those of G; the D chord in measure 11 turns into a
dissonant D⁷ chord (no longer its own tonic expression, now just the
dominant of G); and the boundaries of the measure 11–12 unit are just
the reverse of the boundaries of section 1—D and then G triads in root
position. In all these senses, section 1 seems to be balanced by measures
11–12, and the two fermatas seem clearly expressive of the overall
harmonic action. In this sense, then, the indication "wie oben" directly
after the second fermata seems particularly appropriate—because now

section 2 seems located in measures 11–12, and the final four measures must just be an added confirmation of the restored key.

In considering this overall harmonic shape (G to D and back again), which is projected by the initial fundamental slicing of the music by the fermatas and then, locally, by the other levels of measure groupings, a few points should be made. Notice that some aspects of the D cadence in measure 10 are unsatisfactory. For example, the high G in the voice is unresolved: presumably it is an upper neighbor to the triadic F♯ (although we know that from the perspective of the entire piece it is just an appropriately stressed instance of the tonic pitch class, G). This lack of resolution detracts from the overall effectiveness of D as tonic. Similarly, the fermata in measure 10 actually applies only to the vocal D and the piano treble notes. So although a root-position D triad is struck, a less stable item is sustained. Compare this with the second fermata: the sustained chord is the *entire*, firm root-position G triad. This comparison succinctly demonstrates the subordination of D to G, for, in the long run, the D tonic is just a step between the two extreme G tonics (with the overall progression, of course, describing just the skeletal fifth of the G triad: G–D–G; review here the clear subordination of *B* to *G and D* in section 1).

Before considering the four-bar "coda," we will profit by a study of the melody, which, like the harmony, receives its summarizing affirmation in the last four measures.

In the course of the analysis thus far we have already had the opportunity to study selected portions of the melody grammatically, viewing segments of phrase 1 in terms of the G triad and segments of phrase 2 in terms of the D and b triads. Since in previous analyses we have been developing experience in the local triadicity of tonal melodies, we will now turn directly to a consideration of this melody line from the broader viewpoint of the entire piece.

The first phrase, as we know from our initial ground-level slicing, proceeds by two two-measure groups. The first of these accomplishes the move B–A; these are the first and last notes, the longest (including the fact that the B essentially lasts two beats), and also—as an incidental summary—the *final* two. This incomplete motion seems to generate the entire melody. For the A only weakly returns to B in measure 3, and certainly doesn't move on to G (rather, the line reverses direction locally and moves all the way up to the higher G). But in the second phrase we see the B once again moving to the A over the course of the first two-measure unit. This time there is a skip up from the A, and that portion of the register is abandoned altogether (the following music dipping down as far as A♯, but never quite reaching A). Once in this higher register we must turn our attention away from the B–A line, just as we withdraw from local consideration of the home-base triad.

But after this sally into higher regions is through, and with the return to the earlier tonality, we pick up directly with this same A (measure 11). Once again, it neither convincingly moves back into B (it does so only locally and weakly), nor moves on to G; rather, it once again moves up, and again all the way to the upper G (which serves, in a sense, to "resolve" the high G of measure 10, which is unresolved *in the D-cadence context*, but is restruck here in a G context).

Then in the final two measures of voice music the upper G is brought down an octave. This low G, on the downbeat of measure 14, is the first such pitch in the line, and can finally resolve the long-at-issue A. Then, as if in summary of the entire progress of the line, the final three notes are struck: B–A–G. Thus, we can view the entire line as a gigantic arpeggiation of an interval of the home-base triad; the interval is then filled in with a scalar passing tone. Because the composition is so brief, it is interesting to learn to hear the melody directly in terms of this inferable background structure. We can learn to hear the first two-bar unit as a set-up for the long-range issue; we can listen to the use of repeated eighth notes (the A's of measure 3 relating to the B's of measure 1, for example, and certainly picked up by the repeated A's in measure 11).

Finally we can turn our attention to the little coda, which adds some graceful touches to the already complete harmonic picture (the original tonic having been firmly restored at the second fermata) while it simultaneously *completes* the motion in the voice line.

A harmonic surprise begins this last four-measure group: the unique appearance of the subdominant, which occupies measure 13 in both parts. The composition has been free of this harmony thus far, and its appearance at this late point introduces a typical IV–V–I cadence, which can serve as the kind of G affirmation we are seeking after the rather hasty restoration of that key after only two measures (in measure 12). Note that, for purposes of key establishment, the progression IV–V–I introduces all diatonic degrees, neighbors all tonic-triad pitches in a complete manner (see the composition of chapter 1), and sandwiches the tonic between two symmetrical fifth-distant triads. The appearance of I_4^6 on the downbeat of measure 14 should not be interpreted as an interruption in the IV–V–I progression, since the $_4^6$ formation can be viewed as a neighbor-displaced version of the V chord (which follows directly in the music).

Next, of course, the piano just picks up with an embellished repeat of the final vocal phrase. Two interesting summarizing elements occur here. First, we find that the tune has been changed slightly: the final B–A–G of the voice (which served to summarize the overall melodic motion from the initial B through the persistent A into the final G) is reproduced in changed order as A–B–G. The removal of the A brings the boundaries B and G into direct contiguity, thus summarizing in even more succinct fashion the overall melodic B to G journey.[3]

Second, the C-arpeggio portion of the imitation is harmonized in thirds (a particularly appropriate distance for pairing in light of the fundamental B–G concern; see particularly the parallel thirds between treble and bass in the piano, arising directly from the parallel thirds in the treble at the beginning of measure 14, where the piano B–G third is clearly linked to the vocal B to G summary). This harmonizing changes the sonority of the pure IV chord to that of the complex A–C–E–G, a sound that brings back the chord of measure 2, the first departure from the tonic-triad harmony, and, as such, the first instability in the music.

---

3. That is, we think of the melody as basically describing the triad interval B–G; the A just connects the more fundamental pitches. This is made clear in the piano version, where the A is removed, leaving in isolation the essential interval.

Analysis of Chopin: Mazurka in F, Op. 68, No. 3 (Posth.)

We encounter two new problems in a study of this composition. First of all, we are dealing with a true multisectional piece, one that can be said to have a "form" that is readily recognizable in a first hearing and that obviously structures the listening experience in the most general and pervasive way. While the contrast to the single-surfaced Chopin prelude, Bach invention, and Schubert song is obvious, we will find that this kind of piece can satisfactorily be understood as just a composing-out of the more embedded sectional properties of the works studied earlier. Meanwhile the danger involved in such a case is just one more example, on a much larger scale, of the old labelling problem: all too often the mere accomplishment of simply identifying the overall "form" is taken for analysis, and then serves as an excuse for not looking *into* the content of the sections of the identified form.

The second problem involves "typing" the composition according to its title. After all, the notions we may have about songs, inventions, and preludes are quite vague, and are not likely to prejudice us about events in pieces so titled. But such a title as "Mazurka," which Chopin himself used for some fifty compositions, will tend to hinder analytic discovery because of the screen that the label tends to set up. Much of the richness of such a piece will obviously be lost if we neglect a serious consideration of the rhythm of some notes by merely attributing that rhythm to a "mazurka characteristic." If for the same reason we resist studying the intense peculiarities of the admittedly typical middle section, we will be accepting the piece for much less than it is. Certainly some information about the shared characteristics of mazurkas can be beneficial to the hearing of any one mazurka, but we must be aware of the eclipsing tendency of such information.

One last problem with Chopin's piano music must be mentioned. Because of the composer's occasionally inconsistent treatment of his pieces at various stages of publicational preparation, textual differences exist not only among modern editions, but even between "original" editions and the manuscripts. So some particular dynamic or articulative indication in the version I have used here may not appear in some other edition. Such inconsistencies extend even to Chopin's rhythms, and, given the interaction of pitch and rhythm, we know what analytic problems a contestable rhythm can generate. Clearly, from our awareness of the effect of all the non-pitch elements on our understanding of pitch relations, we can see how an editorial tampering with a composer's intentions is more likely to be destructive than "expressive."

In the most general way, the sixty measures of this piece present a three-section form. At measure 33 and again at measure 45 gross changes in the surface characteristics of the music occur. Aside from the evident changes in key (the F triad being most prominent before measure 33 and after measure 45, the B♭ triad seeming to occupy the intervening measures), the three sections feature obvious differences in speed (fast–a little faster–fast), register (medium–high–medium), texture (contrasts of thickness and thinness), and dynamics (the middle section being exclusively soft, the outer sections mixed). It is in this sense that the contrast with the previous compositions is most explicit. At the same time, we notice not only that all these changes in section 2 are restored to their original style in section 3, but also that section 3 is, with the single exception of the first attack, a literal repetition of the first sixteen measures of section 1. So the overall shape here is very much like that of all the other pieces studied, with an identification between first and last now blown up to the proportion of piecelike areas. Calling this form A–B–A, then, only expresses our awareness of the sectionalization at the surface (including the relation between the outer two sections, which would otherwise be obscured by the designation A–B–C), and refers to no more thorough analytic understanding than does any other first slicing.

Similar considerations of basic contrasts and repetitions lead to a basic slicing of the A section (measures 1–32). The immediate contrast of the loudness in the first eight measures with the softness of the next eight just points up the nearly total repetition that takes place in measures 9–16 (only the final four beats differ from the original). Then eight measures of contrasting music (a different melody, a unique fortissimo, the presence of multiple octaves) connect these two similar statements with a third (measures 25–32, which, with the curious exception of the very first beat, duplicate measures 9–16).

These observations reveal a small a–b–a form within section A, a shape that imitates in miniature the overall format of the piece. The parallel is even more striking when we notice that the closing portion of the first A section, measures 25–32, does not reproduce the entire opening portion, but only the second of the two original (matching) statements—measures 9–16. This sense of truncation is preserved in the larger form also, for the return of A, in measures 45–60, is abbreviated, presenting only the first 16 measures of the first A section. Ex. 7–1 illus-

Ex. 7–1

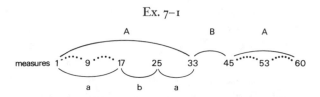

trates these simple and basic relationships. The picture reveals yet another contrast presented by the B section. For the original (immediately repeated) eight-measure unit determines the size of all units (which are either direct repetitions of it, or immediate contrasts between repetitions), with the obvious exception of the B section itself, which is twelve measures in length. (On the other hand this unusual size seems to grow naturally out of the previous norm, since the essential music of section B must be the eight active measures from 37 to 44, with the first four measures of the section just marking time in a bare accompaniment figure. This change in the B section is just the kind of *controlled* change—conditioned by the earlier events out of which the change develops—that we have been looking for in the way of developmental coherence.)

Turning our attention now to the first eight-bar phrase, we find that its overall harmonic accomplishment is to move from the I chord to the V chord, a move presaged by the first two-measure unit. Just as the first eight-bar statement has been seen to be a building block for the entire form, this first separable unit is the obvious building block for the first eight bars, since the unit is the subject of direct transpositional sequencing over the first six measures, with a simple extension of the third block forming the closure of the phrase.

This initial unit presents the F triad (both in the lines and the chordal alignments) in its first measure, and the C triad (momentarily tonicized, with the leading-tone tonic lower neighbor drawn from the C scale) in its second measure. The lines of measure 2 describe intervals of the C triad (E to C, via the passing tone D, in the top line; G to E, by way of passing tone, in the lower treble line, etc.); but the complete lines, over the span of the unit, refer to F: the melody skips within the F triad and then fills in the same skip with passing tones, while the bass arpeggiates the same interval at a different rate but in the same total duration. Such an overall subordination of C to F demonstrates the inclusion of the pitch class C in the F triad, and is a useful miniaturization of the phrase-long spelling-out of the triad interval F–C.

The next version of this unit, in measures 3–4, similarly expresses d minor. And the third and final link in the sequence presents Bb major. In each case the first measure of the two displays the (local) reference triad and the second measure displays the applied dominant in the way originally shown. Some interesting deviations occur in the second of these links: whereas the C expression of measure 2 follows the C scale, the music for D's dominant in measure 4 includes a lowered second degree of a minor; and the choice of mode in both measures seems similarly out of pattern. In both cases, however, the changes seem designed to keep the melody line operating within the original F collection (so C♯ remains C for the a-minor chord; and B, the expected passing tone from C to A, remains Bb, forming the very peculiar sixteenth-note chord in measure 4 which is not like the other dominant-of-dominant types that fill these slots in the other sequence units). And, of course, the choice of d minor (in place of D major) just keeps the pitch class F in circulation (and prevents the challenging F♯).

Now the identity of the dominant of B♭, the subject of the third sequence unit, is the clue to the scheme of transposition that the sequence follows. For the F chord of measure 6, at first seen just as the expected second entry in the local tonic-dominant pattern, closes back to the original tonic F (Ex. 7–2). So we begin hearing measures 5–6 as a I–V

Ex. 7–2

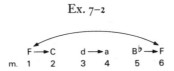

motion in B♭, and then reinterpret it as a IV–I motion in F. This reinterpretation is reinforced by the octave F's in the bass of measure 6 (a slight change in the pattern, adding obvious emphasis to the F), as well as the continued weak-strong alternation of B♭ and F chords that begins at this point.[1] As the motion closes back to F, we can realize that the F triad has now been projected by the succession of sequence endings (C, a, F in measures 2, 4, 6).

The first six measures form an elaborate expression of F in long-range linear ways as well. The lead pitch of the sequence unit is C; the first transposition brings that pitch to A, and the last to F. So the chosen series of transpositions outlines the F triad as the sequence of first melodic pitches in each unit. Furthermore, the F to C motion in the melody of the first unit brings a descending F scale to rest on the triad note C; the second unit continues the scalar motion to the triadic A, and the final version completes the scale to the lower F. Interpreting the melodic D of measure 3 and the similar B♭ of measure 5 as neighbors to triad pitches, we can follow the descending motion along the F scale and interpret each pitch in an overall F context (Ex. 7–3).

These combined and coordinated presentations of the home-base triad account for all of the first eight-bar phrase except the last two measures. As mentioned, measure 7 begins with more F music following the weak B♭ at the end of measure 6; the primacy of F is restored. The phrase now ends by moving to C, by way of the applied dominant G (and, if we read back further and reinterpret, by way of a complete

---

1. It is interesting, in this connection, to return to the first two measures and admit the possibility of hearing the F–C sequence as meaning IV–I in C; after all, to total scale collection here is that of C, not of F, given the presence of B♮.

Ex. 7-3

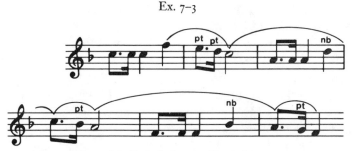

The unlabelled pitches are F-triad tones.

IV–V–I cadence using F as IV!). The lines, also, describe the C-major chord (for example in the upper line, with G–E–D–C operating within the C triad); and the entire tonicization is reminiscent of that of measure 2. The rhythm of this final unit consists of the last four beats of the sequence unit, the same portion repeated to extend the sequence in measures 6–7 (the Bb–F alternation). This metrical orientation (from beat 3 of one measure to the end of the next measure) clarifies the ambiguity stemming from the rhythm in the first sequence unit; in measures 1 and 2 it was unclear whether we wanted to hear the melody in terms of distinct measures (an F interval in measure 1, a C interval in measure 2—thus aligning with the two-measure harmonic motion), or in terms of a cross-over (the F of measure 1 moving to the C of measure 2, presenting an overall F interval). The cross-over form is the one taken seriously by later developments in this first eight-bar phrase, but we will want to remember the original ambiguity, for the issue is subjected to further development in the piece.

The "answer" phrase, measures 9–16, now follows at a contrasting dynamic level. This phrase just repeats all of the foregoing except the cadence, substituting a I cadence for the previous V cadence. This restoration of F completes the "a" section of the a–b–a form that constitutes the large section A, and it is this total F–C–F statement, the first sixteen bars, that is restated at the end of the piece (the final "A" of the overall A–B–A form).

The tonic cadence in measures 15–16 resembles the earlier phrase ending. The third beat of measure 15, corresponding to the third beat of measure 7, is a G-based chord, but now one that remains within the diatonic collection of F. So when this G chord moves to C, as it did previously, it does not bear any tonicizing power, and C is now seen just as the dominant of F. Thus a segment of the cycle of fifths is passed through in this cadence, and the fifth relations among the members of this "chain of dominants" are succinctly demonstrated by the nontriad that is struck on the downbeat of measure 16. For while in traditional terms this chord can be heard as a C chord with D momentarily substituting for the chordal E (to which it immediately moves, in the standard accented incomplete neighbor formation), we can also hear our way *down* the chord, encountering first the interval D–G (suggesting the previous g chord) and then G–C (representing the C chord); so in this way two links in the fifths cycle are stated in one chain-of-fifths attack. (The next expected pitch down the chain would be F, which, of course, appears *next*, and registered just in place!) Additionally, we can even hear the D at the top of the downbeat chord as the result of arpeggiation *out of* the immediately preceding chord.[2]

Finally, we should note the curious accent on the third beat of measure 15. This emphasis has the effect of separating out the cadential unit. But, more than that, it seems connected to the earlier questions of third beat connections (to earlier beats of the same measure, as in measure 1; or to the following measure, as in measures 7–8, and, by reinterpretation, 1–2). Here unquestionably, we think of the music from this third beat to the end of the following measure as constituting one motion. In fact, we may even tend to hear this accented beat as a local downbeat (creating, perhaps, a redivision of the six beats of measures 15–16 into three groups of two each; the cadential chord then just occupies the last "measure" of this cadential "stretto").

F and C, the two principal pitches of the F triad, have so far been the focus of the music. But it is now the remaining triad pitch, A, that receives prime attention in the appropriately "middle" section of the first A section, measures 17–24. The startling triple octave, forcefully attacked, suddenly brings A into prominence. The stability of this pitch class, however, is in question throughout the section, for A is not firmly tonicized. For example, the lack of an immediate triadic context for the octave A contributes to this instability. In the next measure a partial

---

2. And on the surface of the music this skip of a fourth seems to echo all the other such skips, beginning with that of the first measure. This is especially so since the skip is then filled in by steps (at least partially), as have been all such skips so far.

triadic context is supplied, but the C♯–E attacks lack the completing A, and the full A triad on the third beat is not in the stablest inversion. Paradoxically, the E cadence (V of A) in measure 20 goes further to convince us of the tonic status of A than any of the previous A materials. Of course, this E chord comes just halfway through the eight-bar area, and this first four-bar stretch is "answered" by a similar one, which, like the matching parts of the earlier music, supplies a tonic cadence in place of the midway dominant one. But, on the other hand, none of these items is presented very convincingly: the E chord in measure 20 is, like the A octaves, incomplete; and the "cadence" of measure 24 features no dominant, no leading-tone motion.

Unquestionably, this section focuses on A. The point is, the focus clearly lacks emphasis. (Note that the final chord of the section is the only root position A triad, and it is not even complete, lacking the fifth, E; furthermore, it is not given downbeat support.) The "embarrassments" of this section of the piece—the lack of convincing tonic focus, the peculiar "open" fifths and octaves—are due to this studied instability of A, and the entire effect is a contribution to, not a detraction from, the composition as a whole. For with the return of F as tonic in the closing area of the A section (measures 25–32), the overall harmonic movement of the A section becomes F–A–F, a projection of an interval of the home-base triad; while the unstable A does not challenge, but is purposely subordinated to, the fundamental F.

As we leave our study of section A, we should deal with the single peculiarity of the repeat ("a") music: the downbeat C^7 chord in measure 25 is a strange departure from the earlier presentations of the sequence unit. Of course, the dominant seventh functions to introduce the F triad after an absence. But the effect here is to remove the usual stress from the downbeat and place great stress on the second beat. The C^7 chord is weak, dependent, and dissonant; the F chord is just the opposite. Tending to hear beats in terms of their pitch contents, we respond here by shifting the local downbeat focus to beat two; this is especially plausible after the unique fermata at the end of the previous measure (since the un-measured time elapsing between the measures renders uncertain the status of the beat that first enters—for example, the A chord could have been a one-beat chord with a fermata, and then the C^7 would actually be written as an upbeat). The sense of in-place downbeats is immediately restored in measure 26; but the momentary shifting of the downbeat placement is surely reminiscent of the earlier instance of this kind of rearrangement, in measure 15. So, in a sense, we have now had all three possibilities: second-beat downbeats, third-beat downbeats, and of course the usual first-beat downbeats. Since the quick restorations of the mis-placements, in both instances of departure, indicate the ongoing sense of ever-present actual downbeats every three beats, we can easily measure these departures in the pattern of where the "referential," local organiz-ing beat is placed.

Before moving on to study the curious B section, we can quickly dispose of the ultimate A section return. The last 16 bars present the "F" portion of the original A section, the first sixteen measures. Natu-rally, with the subordinated A material omitted, no rounded return is needed within the final A section. The only departure in the repetition, the differing voicing of the initial F chord, can easily be seen to result from the positioning of the dominant seventh that concludes the B section.

We have already specified how the B section is grossly different from the rest of the music. In noting all the peculiar or embarrassing charac-teristics of this section, we should bear in mind how such departures from normal tonal behavior were actually seen to be *positive aspects* of the middle phrase of the A section. That is, we don't want to push aside any abnormalities; nor do we want just to attribute them to some predisposed notion about pieces of this type. Rather, we wish to discover how such details may contribute to the composition.

The open fifths, for example, are not typical tonal sounds. Even less so are the irregularly placed accent marks in the accompaniment (strangely premonitory of a passage in Stravinsky's *The Rite Of Spring*). The harmonic invariance is suspicious (the entire section consisting of the one B♭ harmonic element besides the final two beats of C⁷), as is the metrical orientation (which seems askew because of the treble ac-cents, among other factors). But perhaps strangest of all is the modal quality of the melody, which seems to span the B♭-triad fifth B♭–F, but fills it in with, in addition to normal B♭ scale materials, an inappropriate E♮.

But exactly these peculiarities already ring true in the context of this composition. For the open fifths are surely reminiscent of the (signifi-cantly less striking) open perfect intervals in the middle part of the A section. So a characteristic of an earlier passage (where it has been seen to make sense) now becomes the dominant harmonic feature of a later passage.

The bass accent marks have the effect of obscuring the downbeat functioning of the proper first beats and making downbeat types of other beats: in all, these accents occur on all three kinds of beat. This, then, can be related to the more subtle misplacements of downbeat effects in the A section—the third-beat "downbeat" in measure 15, the second-beat "downbeat" of measure 25. Significantly, the first of these B-section accents appears on a normal downbeat, the standard in the A section against which the special irregularities are measured. So once again, a subtly peculiar element of the earlier music is lifted out and presented full force in a later passage; the earlier events seem to condition or justify the later, more problematic ones. In some of its aspects the B section looks like a sewing together of the most unusual elements of the main body of the piece.

The unusual aspect of the harmony, aside from the open fifths, is the lack of support given the B♭ chord by the melodic materials. The result is, appropriately enough, an even greater instability in the B♭ domain than in the area of the key of A; after all, B♭ is not an F-triad note. But if B♭ is not its own tonic, then what is it? Since it moves directly to C⁷ at the end of the section, and thence into F, we can view the B♭ prolongation as an expression of a subdominant; and the entire B section appears as a IV–V preparation for the ultimate I that is the returning A section. The overall harmonic shape would still seem to be F–A–F, with the B♭ merely a wrinkle in the presentation of the "second" F.

Appropriately, then, the B♭ fifth accompanies a melody made out of *F-scale* materials[3]—for the melodic E♮, in place of *any* instance of E♭, makes the entire circulating pitch collection that of F (the difference between the F and B♭ scales being, of course, just the difference of E and E♭). By this device, tonicization of B♭ (an unwanted effect in the overall plan) is avoided; and at the same time the function of B♭ as sub-dominant of F is hinted at.[4]

---

3. This simultaneous presentation of the worlds of B♭ and F perhaps grows out of the earlier *alternation* of these two triads around measure 6— a unique momentary stasis that brings the previous sequence to a halt.

4. Given the amount of significance we can find in this situation, it should be clear that the weakest explanation—and surely the least interesting and informative, being just a label—would be that the melody and accompaniment are operating in the Lydian form of the B♭ scale.

The result, of course, is a curious mixture of Bb and F elements. The scale is that of F, the chord that of Bb. In the melody itself this confusion is manifest. The skips across the bar line of measures 37–38 describe the Bb triad; but the following pitches, C–E–F, suggest a V–I motion of F (so that the Bb and D lose status, and now seem to be neighbors to C and E). When the melody is rising, the sense of F is clearer, since the E is free to act as a leading tone; on the way down, however, the Bb is reached by way of its own local scale notes, and the focus shifts.

A closer scrutiny of the melody, however, begins to reveal embedded F secrets. Notice, for example, the F triad that concludes the first half of the melody (just preceding a repeat of the opening part of the line). All the melodic accents, also, are F's. And the overall progress of the line is from the initial F to a G a seventh below, which then behaves as a second degree to F, descending firmly into the tonic at the downbeat of the return section, and properly accompanied by a V^7–I progression. In fact, we can even connect these initial and final F's by scalar steps: the E that immediately follows the first F begins the descent and moves quickly to the D at the end of measure 37; C can be located in the next measure, followed by a downbeat Bb (as opposed to an earlier, but weaker, Bb) in measure 39; in measure 40 an A arrives, and then we must wait until the end of the section for the only G. Of course, this structure is not articulated by the surface of the music (except it is curious that some of the notes appear just when needed, and nowhere else in the line), but is only hidden within. On the other hand, the initial detail, the lower grace-note F connected with the upper melodic F, seems to foreshadow the eventual arrival of the end of the descent by associating the boundary pitches at the outset (Ex. 7–4).

We can conclude our discussion by relating this hidden descending F scale to the clearly articulated descending F scale that is carried along by the principal melody in each eight-bar unit where the motive occurs. Perhaps this hidden scale, also lasting eight measures (just the eight-measure melodic portion of the twelve-measure middle section), is just an octave-higher echo of the principal one, which is then stated twice again in its original register.

Carelessly dismissed, the middle section of this composition might indeed seem arbitrary and capricious, or at best just an obligatory characteristic of this kind of piece. Seen as an integral part of the piece, however, it adds immeasurably to the overall coherence and richness

Ex. 7-4

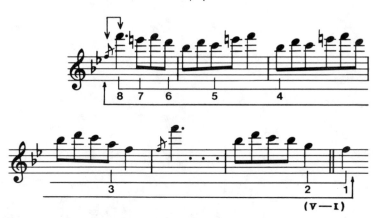

of the composition. Further study of the music of Chopin will confirm that he is a specialist in the "justification" of peculiar details. And in connection with this particular analysis, a study of the Mazurka in g minor (Op. 67, No. 2, op. posth.) is recommended.

Analysis of Beethoven: Piano Sonata in c minor, Op. 13 ("Pathétique"), Second Movement

Here, for the first time, we are dealing with a movement from a multimovement composition. To the extent that such movements usually behave like fairly complete, self-contained compositions in themselves, we can proceed to analyze under the assumption that we are studying another instance of the usual goal-directed tonal structure.

This condition of quasi-independence, however, brings with it the possibility of arbitrary-seeming events and even local incompleteness. That is, some formation in the music may eventually be seen to bear a more satisfactory relationship to some element in a different movement than to its own surroundings; some incomplete motion may find its resolution in a later movement. The sense in which such a movement is just a portion of a larger compositional whole must then place certain reservations on our findings, which would undergo reevaluation should the entire piece be studied.

In practice, however, these possibilities usually resolve themselves into a satisfactory middle position: the movement can be experienced as a sufficient compositional statement, and can then be reexperienced in a richer way when the possibilities of the intermovement relations add new meaning to locally significant details. In the largest sense, for example, we can accept as "given" or arbitrary the choice of key and the shapes of important themes in an isolated movement; these would acquire additional meanings in terms of the entire collection of movements.

In a way, the situation is similar to that encountered in the last chapter, in which the consideration of a multisectional form of a composition brought our investigations of coherence into a larger sphere. In a sonata such as this one, the sense of the participation of a unit in a larger succession of units is just expanded once more.

Seeking a general orientation to the movement, we find the music beginning in very direct fashion. The first eight measures constitute a basic statement, concluding with a break in the bass, a change in register, and the introduction of faster notes. Measures 9–16 confirm the unit status of the first eight measures by generally repeating the same music in a higher octave and with more elaborate accompaniment. Since the conclusion of this second statement in measure 16 is followed by a total break (simultaneous rests in both staves), we think of the first two eight-measure units as forming a larger, separable block.

Then after the intervention of twelve measures of contrasting music (featuring obvious changes in register, texture, rhythm, and tonality), a third statement of the first eight bars appears, ending once again in a thorough halting of the music.

At this point (measure 37) a more drastic change occurs. The minor mode replaces the major, and a completely new theme dominates the activity (that is, is subject to development and restatement, unlike the new melody appearing in the area following measure 17). The dominance of the triplet rhythm further isolates this section.

Finally in measure 51 a return to the opening music begins, including the double statement (in two registers) of the principal eight-bar theme. The movement is concluded by an eight-measure coda that seems to develop out of the immediately preceding materials.

The result of these observations on the gross characteristics of the music is a carving of the movement into three basic areas, the last of which corresponds to the first. Thus, the A section, consisting of the original eight-bar phrase, its octave-higher restatement, a few measures of departure, and a closing restatement, occupies the first thirty-six measures of the piece (just half of the total), and is seen to have its own a–b–a (really a–a'–b–a) internal form, imitating the overall form of the movement. The B section lasts from measure 37 until the return of A in measure 51. And the final A section is abbreviated in comparison with its original (lacking the rounded departure and return, as was the case with the returning A section in the Chopin mazurka), but is then lengthened by the attachment of a brief coda.[1]

Not surprisingly, the opening eight-bar statement is a complex exposition of the Ab-major (tonic) triad, presented both by the lines and the chords into which they align. The linear paths are far from straightforward, however, and we meet our first problem of interpretation in the very first measure of melody.

The chordal C, opening the movement, immediately passes to Bb. The next pitch, however, is a skip away; so the Bb does not directly pass the motion from C to another triad pitch. We can note immediately that the last melodic pitch of the eight-bar phrase, as well as the very last melodic pitch of the piece, is just the Ab to which this Bb can pass, thus filling in an arpeggiated interval (C–Ab) of the tonic triad. (In fact, in both cases—at the end of the phrase, as well as at the end of the piece—the properly registered Ab is directly preceded by a rearticulation of this passing Bb.) Locally, however, the Bb does return motion to C, at the downbeat of measure 3. Meanwhile, the intervening pitch, Eb, functions as a triad reference, and initiates a separate motion through Db into this same C. Since the C of measure 3 is just an eighth note, we may feel that the Bb is not permanently or decisively resolved; then we can compare this to the Bb–Ab resolution at the end of the phrase, where the resolving Ab is essentially a quarter note (in the sense that no melodic pitch succeeds it, the following staccato notes obviously functioning accompanimentally). This initial compositional issue, then, seems to extend over three ranges, on three different levels; the opening C–Bb motion is completed on one level in measure 3, on a higher level in measure 8, and on the broadest level at the end of the piece. Notice in this connection the triple repetition of this Ab in the last measure, as if the ultimate arrival of the Ab were being affirmed. And at the phrase level, the connection may be articulated by the Bb–Ab quarter-note motion (in measure 8), which resumes the even pace of quarter notes established in the first measure (the source of the linear motion) and abandoned first

1. In light of how the identities of the sections were perceived, it seems unwise to refer to the form as, say, ABACA-coda (in which case this ABA refers to our original "A"), for then the more thorough departure represented by the "C" will not be reflected, and B and C will seem like alternate fillers padding a principal succession of A's (standard rondo form).

in the third measure (just where the most local resolution is found, and may be inadequate).

As possible clarification, the interrupting Eb in measure 2 initiates a shape (Eb–Db–C) that imitates the incomplete motion we are studying (C–Bb–[Ab]); and then, immediately upon the conclusion of this imitation, the entire tonic triad is directly arpeggiated, displaying succinctly the overall referential context in which the two linear motions have meaning.

It is just at this point, in the middle of measure 3, that another frustrated motion is introduced. The Ab, ending the triad arpeggiation, moves to Bb; and this new, higher Bb is also unresolved. The next pitch is Eb, representing (linearly) the tonic triad; in both cases of unresolved Bb's, then, the interval Bb–Eb, suggesting the V triad, is stated.

The downbeat Eb of measure 4 passes through the chromatic passing-tone E♮ to its upper neighbor, F (a neighbor motion completed on the next downbeat, with the return to Eb; these three successive downbeats carry the neighbor shape). The Eb then moves to Db (next downbeat), and thence straight down to Ab (including a lower neighbor embellishment, G; and then a resumption of the important last two steps, Bb–Ab, intersecting with our previous description of the lingering Bb problem).

A few extra notes complicate this motion from the fifth (measure 4) down to the tonic (measure 8). The Bb in measure 5 interrupts the large Eb neighbor structure; this Bb forms a fifth with the previous F, thus imitating the Bb–Eb fifth over the measure 3–4 bar line. It then passes directly up to Eb (on the next downbeat), thus producing a third Bb–Eb connection. So our interest in the original Bb, measure 1, is revived, and this appearance in measure 5 serves as a reminder of the unresolved initial Bb. The A♮ in measure 6, then, can be seen to prolong the Bb powerfully, for it supplies that nontriad pitch with its own lower neighbor[2] (resolving technically in the second beat of measure 7; but a resolution is implied by the strong downbeat bb-minor chord in that measure). This prolonged Bb, of course, is directly picked up on the downbeat of measure 8, and finally resolved.

Our study of the melody of the first phrase has revealed a distinct Ab function for each pitch, and a sense of motion *through* the Ab triad

---

2. At the same time, the A♮ creates a fifth with the previous Eb, in yet another imitation of the downward-fifth skip.

Ex. 8–1

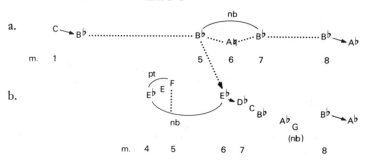

on at least two simultaneous levels (Ex. 8–1). These two lines intersect at various points. The final Ab, of course, is the goal of both motions, and the concluding Bb–Ab step is common to both. The resolution of the important Bb neighbor formation (measures 5–7) is embedded in the descent from Eb to Ab in measure 7. Most important, however, the prolongation of the unresolved Bb is enmeshed with the Eb–Ab strand, since the initial Bb is linked up with an Eb (over the measure 2–3 bar line), and then the reappearance of Bb (and its neighbor, A) starting in measure 5 creates imitating fifths; see particularly the direct connection of Bb and Eb by passing tones (shown by the dotted arrow between the diagrams).

These two intertwined structures thus account for all pitches of the line except those of measures 2–3, where the Eb initiates the local imitation of the C–Bb–Ab motion, and the C begins a simple triad arpeggiation. The only pitch left unaccounted for is the unresolved Bb of measure 3. It is this lack of resolution that directly motivates the octave-higher restatement of these first eight measures; for the second phrase, beginning in measure 9, begins with just the C that is capable of picking up and resolving this maverick Bb.

The bass line of the first eight measures also moves through the Ab triad with Ab materials, and is similarly "polyphonic" in its rich interweaving of structural strands. The opening even succession of bass notes (Ex. 8–2) seems to project part of the tonic triad (the same interval, Ab–C, at issue in the long-range melodic motion begun above it) with the G as neighbor to the Ab's and the Db as incomplete neighbor to the C. But, taking the slur into account, we may hear the progress from Ab to G as the first portion of downward motion from the Ab (thus parallel-

Ex. 8-2

ing the C–Bb downward progress in the melody). Like the Bb of the melody, the bass G may locally resolve back into Ab but also proceed downward in a more long-range sense. This is just what happens in measure 3: the faster motion brings the triadic Ab down through passing tones G and F into the next triad station, Eb, at which point the motion slows down again. Here the curious F octave seems to split this voice into two lines an octave apart, and both F's arrive at Eb's in measure 4. We can then trace the progress of this fifth degree down into the tonic at the end of the eight-bar period. Both Eb's move to the passing-tone Db's in measure 5. Then the two descents behave independently, for only the upper Db moves to the triadic C; but the Bb, on the downbeat of measure 7, is located in the *lower* voice, and moves directly into Ab. This final Ab is once again octave-split, providing possible goals for both motions. Meanwhile, the F in measure 6, bounded by fifths, is the midpoint between elements of the two descents (which, originally one, appear now as one again, but in a different sense—divided between the registers), as well as a long-range neighbor to the triadic Eb in measure 7 (from, perhaps, the Eb in measure 4).

Though the verbal description of the bass activity may seem overburdened with reservations, the general triadic functioning of the passage seems clear, with all nontriad tones relating directly to Ab-triad pitches, and with a general filling in of arpeggiated triad intervals providing the overall context. A tolerance for such local ambiguity is even more necessary for an understanding of the middle line of this first phrase; for here again the tonic triad relevance of all pitches is clear, but we must continually allow for the splitting off of the line into various subsidiary pathways (some even moving into the principal treble or bass lines).

Even at the outset the middle line looks like two simultaneous linear paths (constantly arpeggiated back and forth into a single succession of pitches). The initial Ab and Eb sixteenth notes open up lines that can be traced with little difficulty as long as we allow for the off-shooting into other lines, mentioned above, and for the switching of relative positions within the middle-line complex, which we will witness. The Eb, for example, is a constant "accompaniment" to the higher portion of the middle line, and this repeated E♭ ceases just in time to hook up with the upper bass F in measure 3! So we see the splitting of the bass line into its two octaves as fitting in with the middle line, whose E♭ gives rise to the neighbor F, which then resolves back to E♭ in the bass voice on the downbeat of measure 4.

Meanwhile, the A♭, in the upper portion of the middle line, moves in measure 1 to the neighbor G, back to A♭ on the next downbeat, up to the balancing neighbor B♭, and back again to A♭ on the downbeat of measure 3. From that point the A♭ passes up through scale tones to, actually, the E♭ of the treble voice (downbeat of measure 4; the D♮ is of course a departure from the scale, and will have to be considered shortly). As this portion of the voice passes up into the melody and disappears (just when the lower portion disappears into the bass voice!), another line seems to start with the A♭'s at the end of measure 3 (which clearly grow out of the upper portion of the middle line at the beginning of the measure). This line proceeds from A♭ to the neighbor G (which in measure 5 manages to become the upper part of the middle line), and back again (on the downbeat of measure 6). Simultaneously, this A♭ of measure 3 (last beat) splits off to the B♭, which then moves out into the treble voice (just as the lower part of the middle voice becomes the upper part). An E♭, assuming the role of triad pitch for the lower part of the voice in the latter half of measure 5, generates a neighbor structure (E♭–F–E♭) over measures 6–8; this motion also switches position (from bottom to top) in the middle voice. The downbeat A♭ of measure 6 simultaneously resolves the G and B♭ of measure 5, just as these notes *arose* from A♭, and seems to pass right out of the middle voice (into the A♮, and perhaps back again to A♭ in the melody, since we were viewing the melodic A♮ as a neighbor to B♭, which in turn resolves to A♭). Finally C, in the latter half of measure 6, initiates one last lower-part motion for the middle voice—moving to the neighbor D♭ and back again. These paths, intertwined as they are, are straightforward in design and function, and can be pictured as in Ex. 8–3. Note that all nontriad tones are passing tones or neighbor tones, and everything is understandable in terms of the pitches and intervals of the A♭ triad.

So we see that the lines of the first phrase expose the fundamental tonic triad, and that the two outer lines move *through* the triad in a directed way. These lines are matched to produce chords that likewise

Ex. 8-3

Eb (of upper voice)

D

C

Bb Bb Bb

Ab Ab Ab Ab Ab Ab Ab (into melody A♮)

G G G G

Eb Eb Eb Eb Eb Eb Eb Eb Eb F Eb

(into bass F)

C Db Db C

m. 1   2   3   4 5 6   7 8

prolong or express the tonic triad; all such alignments produce either the
Ab triad itself, or some stack of embellishments to it. Thus, on the largest
level, the phrase moves from the first root position Ab chord to the last
(with the bass note an octave lower and the melodic pitch changed: see
the outer chords of the Chopin prelude for comparison). These two
posts seem well connected by the root-position dominant that occurs
near the midpoint (on the downbeat of measure 4), as announced by
the change in dynamics. This important Eb chord, then, is locally tonicized: it is appropriately supplied with its own dominant (the immediately preceding Bb⁷ chord), and own local scale. Thus we see the reason
for the D♮ in measure 3, even though it is also used as a passing tone
within an Ab interval (Ab to Eb, between the middle and upper voices).

On a more local (chord-to-chord) level, similar alternations of the
I and V chords occur. In the first measure an Ab chord gives way to a
dominant seventh, which is then resolved on the next downbeat by
another tonic chord. Another Eb chord then links this Ab chord to a
third tonic chord, on the next downbeat. The tonic chords on the downbeats of measures 1 and 3 are in root position, while the one on the intermediary downbeat is in a less stable form. So, on a level somewhere between the largest (the overall connection of the initial and final Ab
chords in the phrase) and the most local (the single chord succession),
two stable tonic chords are connected by one of lesser quality; these
are then linked by dominant alignments.

The Ab chord on the downbeat of measure 3 moves directly to
another V chord within the same beat; but this Eb chord is the one about
to be tonicized, since it will form the essential link between the initial
and final Ab chords of the phrase. So this offbeat Eb chord is followed

by a chain of fifth-related chords leading directly back to the E♭ chord on the downbeat of measure 4 (this time, as we have seen, with its own dominant). The quickened harmonic rhythm (one chord per half beat, rather than the previous one chord per beat) seems to carry along the motion into a new local reference chord.

But this established E♭ triad is, after all, just an embellishing structure for the more fundamental A♭ triad to which it returns by the end of the phrase. So this E♭ triad is immediately rendered dissonant; the D once again becomes D♭ (hence the scale collection turns back to that of A♭), and this D♭ is added to the E♭ chord to form the dissonant dominant-seventh chord on the downbeat of measure 5. An entire measure of V⁷ resolves back to the tonic triad on the downbeat of measure 6, but this chord is, again, not in root position; so a definitive restoration of the local A♭ focus is not yet presented.

Meanwhile, with an E♭–C interval link, the A♭ chord becomes F⁷, for a momentary motion to the b♭-minor triad (the underpinning of the prolonged B♭ passing tone, as discussed earlier). To work back to a final A♭ cadence, the dominant (E♭) is now struck; since this dominant follows the B♭ chord, and since B♭ was preceded by *its* dominant, a new chain of dominants is set up, reminiscent of that leading up to the tonicized E♭ of measure 4. In the first chain of dominants, however, the only real dominant relationship (including a leading-tone motion) was that leading directly to the local focus, E♭. Here, however, with the F chord supplying a true dominant (with leading tone) for the B♭, we have the disturbing interruption in the course of the motion back to A♭. The ultimate arrival at home is all the more satisfying. The dissonance toward the end of measure 7, the result of clashes between accented passing tones (C and A♭) and proper E♭⁷ chord tones (E♭ and D♭) further motivates the ultimate cadential closure, as does the similarly produced dissonance on the downbeat of the cadence measure itself (with the V⁷ stack of neighbors appearing simultaneously with the "pedal" A♭, the root of the chord being neighbored by these accented pitches (Ex. 8–4).

Our view of this phrase now corresponds to the two-dimensional tonic-triad prolongation of the sort we have been developing in other tonal pieces. We have a sense of the directed motion of the pitches in the unit, and also a sense of nonresolution: for the marked B♭ at the end of measure 3 needs a tonic triad pitch to resolve it (especially if the curious phrase line that leads *to* this B♭, but then leaves it hanging, is

Ex. 8-4

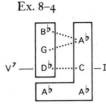

measure 8:   beat 1   beat 2

Eb, common to both chords, is also present; the dotted lines show the neighbor connections, the neighbors aligning to form the V⁷.

performed). The second eight-bar unit then comes to elaborate on the first. It picks up from this hanging Bb, and exposes the tonic triad in a new register. The connecting figure, triplets that bridge the two registers, is purely the Ab triad, the structure that is the subject of the music of the two registers.

Of course, if measures 9–16 replay all the issues of the first eight measures, another unresolved Bb will be left hanging at the end of this phrase; indeed the Bb of measure 11 leads the way into the third phrase (our middle area of the A section) just as the previously unresolved (lower) Bb motivated the appearance of the second, repeating phrase.

The triple-octave climb that begins the next phrase is thus closely knit to the two preceding phrases. For the first (thirty-second-note) C (pickup to measure 17) recapitulates the first melodic pitch of the piece; the second C brings back the corresponding first pitch of the second phrase; and the third, highest, C completes the pattern (actually, brings it "up to date") by resolving the Bb of measure 11 (as the C on the downbeat of measure 17 relates to an earlier Bb resolution). Moreover, the steadily rising figure, connecting all the registers, is reminiscent of the triplet phrase connection in measure 8.

And though the tonality seems new, the lone C can at first be heard just in terms of the Ab triad; in fact, when the Ab enters in the melody, the interval (C–Ab) thus formed melodically and harmonically can still be thought of in terms of the old tonic focus. By the time the measure is complete, however, the skip away from F shows that G passes the motion not *through* F to some triadic Eb, but to F itself. F minor seems like the new triadic focus, and of course shares with the previous tonic structure two-thirds of its content (Ex. 8–5).

But the new section is tonally ambiguous: whereas in the earlier

Ex. 8-5

E♭

C ⋯⋯⋯C

A♭⋯⋯A♭

F

music a single referential element (the A♭ triad) was seen to provide meaning for all the pitch events (including, of course, their rhythmic embodiment), here such a focus is lacking. And, as we have seen, this is a desirable situation; for the instability motivates a return to the tonic triad's domain—the rounding out of this A section with a repeat (measures 29–36) of the first eight bars.

The f-minor focus is unsteady because, first of all, the triad is introduced in a very weak manner. Not until the end of measure 17 is the entire triad present, and then only in the dissonant $^6_4$ position. The even alternation of f and its true dominant, C, over the first three measures of the section tends to clarify the focus; but, again, the dominants occur on the downbeats, the "tonic" on the weaker third beats. In fact, when next the f chord moves by another such dominant-type motion to the B♭ chord of measure 20, and then that B♭ chord is altered to become an embellishing diminished-seventh chord (end of measure 20), the c-minor triad seems to receive a tonic's emphasis (downbeat of measure 21)—for the diminished-seventh chord acts like a dominant for C. We then might want to reinterpret the earlier f–C alternations in favor of a C focus (that is, a plagal inflection of C)![3]

But C proves not to be the focus either; for, starting with the latter half of measure 21, a clear cadential motion into E♭ is begun. The first chord of this motion looks like a combination of the A♭ and f triads (the F–A♭–C portion of the four-pitch chord being used for the melody, the A♭–E♭ portion in the bass). So this chord combines the initial chords of the two sections (measures 1 and 17), and leads the way into the focus of the second section, E♭. For the A♭ portion of this chord behaves like a subdominant for a IV–V–I cadence in E♭; while the f portion behaves

3. It might even be interesting to go back and hear the lone C in measure 17 as the root of a C triad. For the pattern of alternating C and f chords, changing every half measure, would be consistent with that interpretation. Of course with the previous E♭ in our thoughts and the dissonant form of C in measure 19, such an interpretation is largely fanciful.

like a supertonic, for a ii–V–I (cycle-of-fifths) motion into Eb. The function of the initial f chord (measure 17) as ii of Eb is now clear, with the direct resolution of the pitch F (measure 21, melody) by the pitch Eb (downbeat of measure 23; these two pitches are isolated by a variety of means, and are restated as the last two pitches of the cadential melody). In retrospect, then, we can view the anticipation figure on Eb (over the bar line between measures 20 and 21) as a preparation of the tonicization to come; and the Bb⁷–c motion over those measures now appears as a V⁷–vi (deceptive) cadence in Eb (with the ultimate tonic pitch, Eb, used just as the third of another chord—but uniquely substantiated by the anticipation figure).

At this point the middle phrase comes to a temporary halt—an articulation of the establishment of its tonal focus. Dominant–tonic motions in this key, with increasing chromatic inflection (related, perhaps, to the original chromatic passing tone, the E in measure 4), confirm the focus (see the second stopping point in measure 25, and the sustained Eb chord in measures 27–28). But by the end of measure 28 one more chromatic passing tone, the Db at the end of a voice that already renders the Eb chord unstable (see, for example, the un-tonic-like lowered second degree, Fb), changes the Eb chord to an Eb⁷, ready to return to the Ab home base, from which, we now see, it has arisen. The return to the opening music coincides with the restoration of the background tonic, and the overall harmonic shape of the A section (Ex. 8–6) becomes clear. This

Ex. 8-6

	I	V	I
	Ab	Eb	Ab
m.	1	23	36

essential motion of course follows the defining skeletal fifth, Ab–Eb, of the home-base triad, and it can be seen as just a higher level manifestation of the same structure seen over phrase one (measures 1 to 4 to 8), as well as locally (for example, over the course of the first three beats of the piece). And on each level the sense of stability associated with the Ab music and instability associated with the "connecting" Eb music is preserved: the dissonant quality of the Eb chord in measure 1, connecting two stabler Ab chords; the just temporary tonicization of Eb in the middle of phrase one; the troubled presentation of Eb tonality in this middle

phrase (note all the dissonant on-the-beat elements, due to the purposeful misplacement of passing and neighbor tones in relation to the local
chords: the Eb on the downbeat of measure 24, the F on the downbeat
of measure 27, etc.). In each case the Eb instability motivates the Ab
return, and this is most marked throughout the middle phrase. The Eb
tonic is established only very gradually, and then dissolved very quickly;
and though we can, once we acknowledge the function of Eb, begin
to interpret many of the lines according to the Eb triad, we can also see
the seeds of motion into Ab already at work in the Eb music: as just
one example, note the low Bb of measure 24 (reappearing two measures
later) acting as long-range upper neighbor to the reinforced Ab in measure 29.

   The unified functional unit of these first 36 measures now gives way
to the large middle section that joins the A section to its truncated repeat at the end of the movement. The sense of instability associated with
the abandonment of local tonic activity is even greater in this B section,
and brings up to one final level the arched form experienced at all lesser
levels (and seen once again over the course of the entire sonata, with
this middle movement as connector of two more fundamental tonal
expressions). The pervasive triplet characteristic of this section can now
be seen to derive most clearly from the original triplet music in measure
8; for that original figure served just as a connector of two Ab phrases,
and this middle section of triplet music is essentially just a connector of
two large-scale Ab *sections*.

   The new section begins in ab minor, the tonic triad of which forms
the referential basis for the lines and chords in the first five measures.
But the same music repeats in the key of E major starting in measure 45;
the apparent link between these two seemingly distant triads is the
shared interval Ab (=G♯) − Cb (=B) (Ex. 8–7). So the tonic pitch,

Ex. 8-7

E♭

C♭............B

A♭............G#

E

Ab, is really the link *within* the middle section, as well as between the
large sections (Ex. 8–8). In fact, the strange E triad seems quite normal

Ex. 8-8

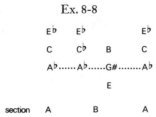

| section | A | B | A |

when we view it as a neighbor structure to the A♭ triad. The clue is the gradual development of the E triad out of the original tonic triad: first the C (of the A♭ triad) is lowered by half step to C♭ (=B), thus forming the a♭-minor triad with which the middle section begins; then, if the E♭ (the only other remaining original note that can change, if the A♭ is to remain constant throughout the process) is raised by the same half-step measure, the result is E. The neighbor relation between the two triads is thus developed in two distinct stages, and is summarized in Ex. 8–9. (Once again the pronounced E♭–E♮ in the melody of measure 4 comes to mind!)

Ex. 8-9

The switch into the key of E is of course the greatest sign of instability in the middle section. (The middle phrase of the A section at least developed and then abandoned one local tonic; here one focus is traded for another.) The sforzando effects on the embellishing dominant chords in measures 42 and 43 just emphasize the strangeness of the change, for the B⁷ chord in measure 42 must surely be puzzling to us until the establishment of E is presented several measures later.[4] Then the resumption of the middle-section theme, together with the unassuming pianissimo (measure 45), is rather humorous in its offhand treatment of the change that has just taken place.

4. At the same time, the sharing principle is in evidence again, with the interval B–D♯ enharmonically shared by the B⁷ and the (immediately preceding) a♭-minor triad.

The same dynamic accents reappear to mark the destruction of the E center. The next such accented item (measure 48) is the tonally ambiguous diminished seventh,[5] which immediately confuses the sense of focus. Once again, however, the link between the E chord and this one is the shared interval Cb–Ab. By successive half-step lowerings, the notes of this diminished seventh come to form an Eb^7 chord, ready to resolve directly into the Ab chord that marks the beginning of the recapitulation, measure 51. Thus we see that the Cb–Ab interval has been prolonged throughout the length of the B section, finally moves to its lower neighboring interval Bb–G, and returns into the Ab-major triad at the beginning of the next section (Ex. 8–10). The interval Ab–Cb seems to be

Ex. 8-10

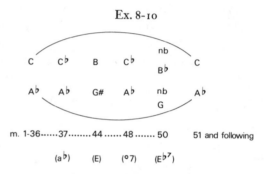

(in addition to other things we have said about it) the middle-section "version" of the more basic Ab–C interval. Tonally the middle section appears as a wrinkle in the overall Ab–triadic surface. Its surface formations and characteristics, too, relate to aspects of the earlier music, and items such as the switches in registral positioning of the melodic action (see measures 37–41, etc.), the downbeat appoggiatura-type dissonances (as in measure 40), and the chromatic action of certain motions (as in measure 38) should be related to their sources in the A section for a fuller understanding of the unity of the composition.

Our final A section returns, now tainted by the pervasive triplet characteristic of the middle section (ironically, originally derived from the earlier A section). Perhaps the unresolved high Bb of measure 61 (the equivalent of which in the first A section was seen to motivate the middle

---

5. Since all the intervals in the diminished seventh are of the same absolute (in semitones) size, no focus or root can be ascribed; the chord must take its meaning from surrounding tonal events.

phrase, with the high C of measure 18 being the key pitch) now suggests the appearance of a coda phrase to round off the movement. If so, this B♭ is not, like all the previous ones, resolved up to the triadic C, but down to A♭ (downbeat, measure 70). There is further evidence that the coda is not just an arbitrary closing addition, but has been wisely fashioned to resolve and recapitulate previous details. For example, when the coda tune of measures 67–68 is restated an octave higher (in measure 69), the important octave-higher repeat of the first eight bars (in the second eight bars) is surely echoed. Even the E♭–E–F detail that is the "motive" of the coda melody obviously quotes that sequence of pitches from measures 4–5. And the repeated coda cadence, putting to rest all previous V–I issues, takes place in two registers an octave apart: measures 71 and 72. Thus the octave rise over the first sixteen bars is finally brought back down here in the coda, with the final A♭ appearing in a kind of "obligatory" register (as suggested at the outset in terms of an *overall* connection between the *first* C and the *last* A♭).

Finally, just a word about the general relations between movements of this sonata, with regard to a minute detail at the end of the slow movement. The high D♭ of measure 69 is technically not resolved in the movement (compare the same pitches, G–D♭, in measure 38, and the quick resolution of the D♭ by the triadic C♭ in the next measure). If we expect either a C or an E♭ (the neighboring tonic triad pitch classes) to pick up this D♭, it is comforting to know that just these two pitch classes form the intersection of tonic triads between the movements of the sonata (which is in c minor) (Ex. 8–11). We can thus expect C and E♭ to appear

Ex. 8-11

G		G
E♭ .... E♭		E♭
C .... C		C
	A♭	
movement: 1	2	3

in every kind of important role in the movement that follows this one; perhaps one such instance of one of these notes will be suitable for a connection that we may seek to this D♭.

Analysis of Mozart: Piano Sonata in G, K. 283, First Movement

The "sonata form" with which most listeners are familiar is such a useful generalization of the surface behavior of so many classical and romantic first movements that it would be pointless to deny its relevance here, even in light of all the previous emphatic dismissal of such labels. The general convention represented by this form apparently helped composers write longer pieces, as it helps us listen to them. Lasting 120 measures, this movement is the most extensive complete unit we will study in this volume; it is obviously convenient to be able to refer to areas of the movement in terms of an assumed common notion about the overall shape of the music.

We will expect, then, that the music will follow this basic plan: two contrasting subjects (in, respectively, the tonic and the dominant) form a separable expositionary area; a development section, characterized by the usual middle-section instabilities, makes further music out of elements of the exposition; and a recapitulating section restores the original key and restates the exposition materials. *Except for the two-part nature of the exposition, this scheme appears just as a generalization of all the "forms" we have witnessed in previous studies.* And, as in those smaller examples, this form has as its chief purpose the projection over the course of the piece of the tonic triad; for the two themes of an exposition merely formalize the notion of moving from tonic to dominant (thus describing an interval, 1–5, of the tonic triad); and the return to the recapitulation completes the harmonic motion. Encountering at last a classical sonata-form movement, we see that it represents just another, larger level on which triad-induced shapes are projected.

As usual, the music begins by announcing its own tonic triad. The first notes of melody and accompaniment separately and together outline the G triad; but, more importantly, the first phrase (as defined by the unified surface of the first four measures, including the initial pickup, but—in direct balance—excluding the pickup to measure 5) prolongs this triad. Vertically, the alignments of voices clearly suggest the progression I–V⁷–I; linearly, all paths elaborate pitches of or move through intervals of the I triad. Thus the triad is presented in the usual two-dimensional way.

The typical Alberti-bass formation, like the middle voice of the first eight bars of the Beethoven movement, can be seen as a combination of various interwoven structural strands. Were elements of such strands struck simultaneously, a typical block-chordal formation would result (see for example the Chopin prelude). The path through the accompaniment figure that is heard as the succession of downbeats (metrically stressed notes) as well as lowest notes in each metrical grouping describes an elaboration of the tonic pitch, G: G–A–F♯–G; the concluding G is repeated at the end of its group, and punctuates the end of the statement. The top notes of the accompaniment just sustain the triad pitch D. Meanwhile the middle line of the bass music parallels the lowest part by forming a neighbor group around the triad pitch B: B–C–A–B. The arpeggiation of the chords formed by these conjoined lines results in the single, presented succession of the bass part (Ex. 9–1), with all lines

Ex. 9-1

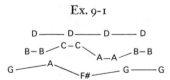

following G-significant paths and joining to outline G-significant chords.

It is fortunate, for the fate of the piece, that the tune line is a good deal less regular; for we shall see how the peculiarities of the melody in this first phrase seem to generate a great deal of the detail and general behavior of the remainder of the movement. After a triad interval (D–B) is exposed, the remaining triad note, G, is introduced; it moves immediately to its lower neighbor, F♯, which does not, however, return to G (or, alternatively, pass through E to the triadic D) within the span of the four-bar phrase. With a surprising jump into a higher register, two more nontriad pitches, A and F♯, spontaneously appear (in motivic imitation of the opening particle); they also do not resolve into the tonic triad in the phrase. Finally the C in measure 3 appears as an incomplete upper neighbor to the triadic B (although it may arise from the initial D, as a long-range passing tone to the B, thus connecting over the *span* of the phrase the interval, D to B, with which the phrase *began*), and the original registral position of the phrase is restored along with the return to the tonic triad.

Though the melody of this first statement contains much that is unsettling (the unresolved nontriad pitches, the jumpy registral disposition), it is yet rather satisfying as a unit. The rhythmic sense of anacrusis (third beat to first beat) is sustained throughout; the overall harmonic motion of triad–nontriad–triad (aligning with the bass) is nicely rounded by the end of the phrase; the two outreaching registral positions (as represented by the low F♯ and the high A) neatly sandwich the first (and last) registral positions; and the intervals minor third and semitone appear in a motivic pattern (third–second–third–second). The weaving together of the instabilities into this rather stable and unified context thus produces an opening statement that is both definitive and generative.

The second phrase, starting with the melodic pickup to measure 5, effectively deals with some of the issues raised by the first phrase. The initial high G in the melody resolves both the previous A and F♯ of that register. This G then begins a slow arpeggiation of the triad interval G–D (completed in measure 7, as marked by a skeletal summary of the motion, followed by a repetition of the concluding pitch, D), filled in by scalar passing tones. This motion from G to D seems to connect smoothly two of the registral areas of the first phrase: the high G represents the upper portion of the first phrase by resolving the A and F♯, while the D obviously refers to the "middle" register of the first phrase (being the same note with which the piece begins). The remainder of the melody in the second phrase (which clearly extends up to the G cadence in measure 10, the point where motion stops and a repeat begins) consists of a large scalar passage in sixteenths, which also connects D with G (now in the opposite order), and seems to join the two upper registers with the lower one (the passage reaches just down to and concludes with the G and F♯ found in the first two measures of the piece). Finally, the unresolved low F♯ of measure 2 can be seen to be picked up and resolved by the G in the bass part on the downbeat of measure 5. (Though this G is "misharmonized"—by the C triad, rather than the G triad—the same G is repeated on the next downbeat, in the "proper" context.)

These features of the second phrase support the impression that it is a direct consequence of the opening phrase.[1] In fact, the extension into six measures is brought about in a highly controlled derivation from the first phrase. Both phrases begin with pickups and proceed to tonic cadences on the downbeat of their fourth measures. But the second phrase simultaneously initiates new motion (the sixteenth passage) on that cadence downbeat. Harmonically this new motion is just a cadence extension (moving through the subdominant into a I_4^6–V^7–I pattern); this extension is rhythmically peculiar because of the hemiola effect (the downbeat of measure 9 being unarticulated, and the six beats of measures 8–9 appearing as three groups of two each). So the entire shape of the phrase, including the rushed compression into the final cadence, grows out of the shape of the first phrase, along with the details, shapes, and accomplishments of the melodic line.

Meanwhile the second phrase remains solidly in the tonic domain, all lines and chords serving to prolong the tonic triad (including the sixteenth-note passage, each pitch of which can be assigned a clear function within G-interval motions—for example, the A on beat 3 of measure 9 passing from the B on beat 2 to the G on the next downbeat; the notion of incomplete neighbors will help account for some pitches in the lower lines). The harmonic plan for the phrase is I–IV–I–V^7–I, starting with the tonic pickup to measure 5 and concluding with the G chord on the downbeat of measure 8 (where the cadence extension begins; the cadence itself takes the form of the same succession of chords—a series that seems to expand upon the harmonic outline of the first phrase).

Next the third phrase repeats the music of the second, starting off in

---

1. We can learn to hear the new phrase as beginning with an augmented echo of a detail that ends the old phrase: compare the upper-staff quarter notes C–B (measures 3–4) with their equivalents an octave lower in downbeat half notes (measures 5–6).

a lower octave but switching to the higher octave after two measures. Again the multiple register format relates to the switching of register in miniature in the first phrase. In fact, the initial G–F♯ of phrase three quotes exactly the G–F♯ in the first phrase, the notes that introduced the "low" treble register.

The next six measures likewise form a phrase unit; so this larger size, as developed out of the initial four-measure size, has established itself as the norm for phrase length. The fourth phrase brings the music into a D cadence in measure 22, after which an entirely new theme is introduced in the dominant. So the first sixteen measures of the piece constitute the "first theme," and the following six measures form a transition into the "second theme." Together these two themes, with their transitional and final cadential material, provide the formal exposition of the movement.

The structure of the transition is, typically, significant for the piece of which it is a part. Melodically it begins with successive thirds, a detail deriving from the first moment of the piece, where the first melodic detail is a third. (In fact, the bass third G–B in measure 1 gives the exact pitches, in the proper register, of the first notes of the transition melody.) These melodic thirds are sewn together by seconds—and this is the other melodic particle of the melody of the first phrase. As the transition proceeds, the positions of these seconds and thirds are switched (for the first time at the beginning of measure 19)—seconds connected by thirds. It will be recalled that the entire first-phrase melody is just a succession of these two intervals (in isolation, so that the intervals *between* them—for example the D–G in measure 1—are not heard nearly as directly) (Ex. 9–2).

Ex. 9-2

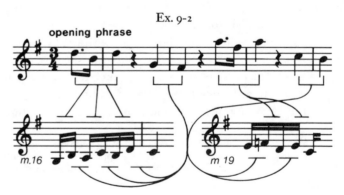

Other melodic and harmonic matters of this transition evidently derive from features of the first theme area. The transition opens with an
arpeggiated linear fourth, G–C (from rest to rest), which sets up a rising
fourth pattern; perhaps this is related to the gradually descending scalar
fourth from G *down* to D over measures 4–7. That original fourth introduced the subdominant harmony, C (measure 5), and here in the
transition this fourth leads the way to a C tonality (complete with
change of scale contents to match). In fact the harmonies emphasized in
the transition (C, G, and the ultimate D) just recapitulate the only harmonies we have had so far. Perhaps we can also relate the doubled-thirds
motion in the treble to the parallel (simultaneous) thirds in the bass of
measures 7–8.

The cadence on D in measure 22 features all the usual surface an-
nouncements, suggesting a fundamental slicing at that point: the quarter-
note octave D's (both vertically and linearly!), the unique trill on D
(not found in some editions), the total silence of a full beat.

The contrasts between the first and second themes are not limited
to tonality. The basically disjunct intervallic character of the first theme
(due to the registral jumps) is replaced by smooth stepwise motion. The
syncopations in measures 23 and 24 and the unusual imbalanced segmen-
tations of the beats (♪♩.) in measure 25 represent apparently new rhythmic characteristics. And the pickup style of the first theme is replaced
here by simple downbeat beginnings. On the other hand, the elaborated
repeat that begins in measure 27 establishes the first four bars of the
second subject as a phrase unit, thus restoring (for the first time since
the very opening of the movement) the four-bar size, and so associating
the two themes. The tonic and dominant areas, delineating the fundamental fifth of the G triad, are thus formalized as contrasting but comparable reference points. (With the ultimate return to the tonic, the overall subordination of dominant to tonic will be manifest.)

Just as the low-register particle in the first phrase seems to generate
later activity in that register (see particularly measures 10–11), the
upper-register detail in the beginning of the piece, A–F♯, can be seen to
give rise to this second theme, which actually begins with this very A,
and goes on to connect that A by step to F♯ (these two notes now being
triad notes, an eventuality perhaps foreshadowed by their powerful isolation in the first phrase).

The new subject seems to spell out its own triad (D) in predictable and simple linear and vertical ways, which need not be specified here, but should be studied for practice; no new problems of interpretation occur. Similarly the elaborated form of these first four measures (beginning in measure 27) is straightforward pitch-wise. But the syncopations of the initial second-subject phrase have been turned into anacrusis-type figures (every offbeat leading into the following beat). Thus the rhythmic features of first and second subjects are here combined into a new rhythmic surface.

The theme of the second-subject area is really complete after this double period of four-bar phrases, and the remainder of the exposition, from measure 31 to the double bar in measure 53, is given over to elaborate cadential statements in the dominant key. Cadential arrivals occur on the downbeats of measures 38, 43, 44, 45, 48, 51, 52, 53 (all V–I motions, with the new tonic always in root position and on the strongest metrical position). These events serve to clarify absolutely the sense of change into the new key, while they take their form from various details and features of the earlier music.

The half-step music starting in measure 31 (immediately following the conclusion of the second statement of the second theme) can be thought of as a grand expansion of the half-step particle from the first four-bar phrase. The harmonic functions of these step-related stacks (all V–I-type pairs) are clear; the essential motion is from I (measures 31–33) through IV (the G chords in measure 34, arrived at by way of cycle-of-fifths chains) to V^7 (downbeat of measure 35, where the surface of the music changes). At this point, the anacrusis effect (of the very first event of the piece) asserts itself for a definitive motion into I (at the downbeat of measure 38). The lack of completion in the treble voice at this cadence motivates the repetition (measures 38–43) of this cadential motion, in which the two-quarter-note anacrusis (over the measure 35–36 bar line) becomes three upbeat eighth notes (in measure 40) reminiscent of that effect at the beginning of the exposition transition, measure 16.

The next cadential motions, beginning in measure 43, surely reflect first the exposition-transition successive thirds connected by seconds (starting in measure 16); next the trill from the end of that transition (measure 22); next the syncopated descending scale from the second subject (compare measures 45–46 with measures 23–24); and finally the three-eighth-note anacrusis (measure 47). The elaborated repeat of measures 45–47, which takes place next in measures 48–50, reflects the second-subject notion of phrase repetition-elaboration (see measures 23–26 and 27–30, as compared with the two sets of three measures here). In this latest elaboration, the diatonically descending scale passages, aligning into $^6_3$ triads, generate local scale usages each step of the way (with each $^6_3$ chord, starting with the b minor on the downbeat of measure 48, elaborated with its own scale); the closing motion of the elaboration (measure 50, treble) seems reminiscent of the sixteenth notes in the last two beats of measure 9.

The final cadential motion is the most direct, and the simple statement of V^7/IV–IV–V^7–I is carried along by the rhythmic feature (three eighth notes leading to a downbeat) that combines the features of the transition pickup (measure 16) and the original rhythmic thrust into the movement (across the first bar line).

These interesting features of the second-subject area are of course embedded in the usual tonal-grammatical context, which, at this stage, we need not consistently make explicit in our discussion, but of which we yet need to be constantly aware.

The impressive silence of two beats (twice the length of the separation between the first and second subjects in the exposition) separates the exposition from the brief development section. Thus the most fundamental slice of the piece occurs at this point (punctuating the overall motion to date from G to D; the remainder of the piece, as second slice, just accomplishes the return motion, D to G[2]). The formal function of the development is to make dissonant (by the addition of a seventh) the local tonic triad D. This function manifests itself through a recasting of certain exposition materials. In this case the development is exceptionally brief and accomplishes its goal in a highly succinct manner. The D triad is temporarily expressed or prolonged by a new theme, which, we shall see, is just a skeletal presentation of the first theme of the exposition; then a transitional passage, also modelled after exposition music, renders the D triad dissonant, and ready to act as dominant seventh to the original (and thus overall) tonic, G.

The development melody begins on a pitch that has been admirably prepared for; the A on the downbeat of measure 54 can be heard in terms of the first (unprepared) A in measure 2, by way of the initial

2. We see then that the three-part form (of exposition–development–recapitulation) is counterpointed with this fundamental two-part form.

melodic pitch of the second subject. This measure-54 A now descends by scale to C♯, the leading tone, a sixth lower. This motion is just that accomplished by the first two particles of the first theme, a unit which likewise starts on the fifth degree and ends on the leading tone, a sixth lower (Ex. 9-3). The relation is hard to detect at first because the out-

Ex. 9-3

ward form has been altered to such an extent, and because the initial and final attack points in the development version differ metrically from those of the expository version.

The matching answering motion in the development theme is even more succinct. In the original source (the first phrase), the second motion connects A (measures 2–3) to B, a seventh lower. Here in the development only the two end points, a seventh apart, are stated (Ex. 9-4). The E then wanders back to A for an elaborated repeat of this four-bar unit (by now an established procedure in this piece).

Ex. 9-4

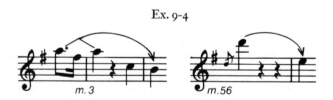

The bass cooperates with this melody in interesting ways. An ascent from D to C♯ takes place in parallel thirds (which perhaps echo those of measures 7–8) over the course of the first phrase of the development; the failure to complete the rise to D contributes to the sense of motivation behind the phrase repetition. In the lower octave version (beginning in measure 58), the octave ascent is complete (in measure 62, with the delayed middle D).

At this point the D, reached in the bass, is sustained as a pedal. Above it is suspended what sometimes appears as a D triad in root position, and otherwise seems like a G chord in $^6_4$ position. In either case, the linear motion in the treble provides great impetus into the tonic G (and the recapitulation). Taking the cadence pitch D on the downbeat of measure 62 (treble) as a springboard, we can see the C on the downbeat of measure 64, the result of the first treble scalar descent in thirds, as the next pitch in a long-range descent that eventually spells out the interval D–G (ending in measure 72). This descent directly connects the two tonalities (that of the development and that of the recapitulation), which are represented succinctly by the end points of the descending interval; but it also describes an interval of the fundamental G triad, thus demonstrating the overall subordination of the D tonality to the G tonality.

The next local scalar descent (the form, of course, is taken most recently from the bass ascent in thirds in the earlier part of the development, but the sources for such activity lie further back in the movement) brings the long-range motion down to B (on the downbeat of measure 66). One more such motion brings the journey to A (downbeat of measure 68), at which point the expected G is delayed. A rising scale prolongs the A (downbeat of measure 69), which descends almost parenthetically to G only after the theme of the recapitulation has slipped in (pickup to measure 72). The principal theme now has a pleasing solidity to its registral behavior. The initial D is just the one used so prominently in measure 62; the lower register begins with the G that grows directly and necessarily out of the gradually descending line at the end of the development; and the high register is opened up by the A that has recently been a principal triad station in that register (measure 54) in the previous key. So, in retrospect, the development not only is justified by the exposition, but can be seen to "justify" the exposition in return!

Once again, many of the grammatical (particularly the harmonic) aspects of the development have been left out of our explicit considerations, in favor of more informal modes of coherence.

Naturally one basic change must be expected in the recapitulation, for if the second subject were presented in its original key (the dominant), then the movement would end in that key, and the entire rounded scheme of G–D–G would crumble. In many cases the transition music between first and second subjects must be reworked in the recapitulation so that the transition brings the tonality not from tonic to dominant, but from tonic back to tonic. In this case, however, the transition can remain as it is, with the D to which it leads acting now just as a dominant to G (rather than, as previously, a tonic to itself). This is so perhaps because this transition brings about no strong D cadence; the D octave that concludes the transitional passage is not enforced with a regular V–I motion, but is approached only linearly, and without harmonic support. The rest that starkly separates the cadence pitch of the transition from the first beat of the second subject further facilitates the double usage of the transition, since there is no melodic connection between that last pitch and the opening of the second subject that must be reworked in order to connect to a newly placed (transposed) second subject.

Other than the fifth-transposition of the entire second-subject area, then, the recapitulation appears as an exact restatement of the exposition, with one curious exception: the two repeated phrases that immediately follow the first (four-bar) theme in the exposition are entirely absent in the recapitulation, and are replaced by a step-higher repeat of the first four bars, which then works its way back to the tonic (at the point where the transition passage begins). The four bars in a minor come as a great surprise, especially since the recapitulation has just begun, and the feeling of security in the newly reestablished tonic key is not yet settled. And yet the transition into a is carefully crafted, with the upper part of the bass music in measure 75 just proceeding through a G-triad interval (D–B), but matched in such a way as to produce B–G♯ (not B–G) on its last attack; this B–G♯ is then interpreted as an interval of the E chord, as dominant of A. So the G♯ is the only surprising pitch, and the entire switch hinges on that note.

The phrase in a, however, may serve a cohesive developmental purpose. For following a four-bar phrase "on" G (in the sense that the G bass pitch on the downbeat of measure 72 initiates the foundation of the passage) with a duplicate "on" A (again, according to the leading bass pitch) simply expands by one level the bass activity of the first two measures of the first phrase (the lead, downbeat notes again being G–A, with the A in the same register, in fact, as the one that initiates the repeating phrase). Furthermore, this expansion from two single measures to two four-bar groups expresses a comparison of the two units (measures, four-measure groups) by which the music may be regulated.

Perhaps even the F chord that follows this a-minor excursion (measure 80) can be understood in terms of this expansion. For the bass motion of the first phrase describes a neighbor formation around G: G–A–F♯–G. Since the larger move to a in measure 76 imitates the A pitch in the neighbor group, perhaps the F chord is meant to be a balancing lower "neighbor chord." A G chord then comes (downbeat of measure 83) to close the "chordal" neighbor group and complete the imitation of the original bass neighbor line.

Analysis of Brahms:
Intermezzo, Op. 76, No. 7,
for Piano

NB: In numbering the measures of this piece we will have to deal with the matter of first and second endings. For convenience we can call the initial alternate pair 16a and 16b; the "*dolce*" measure is then 17. The situation toward the end of the piece is more troublesome, for some editions divide the second measure of the first ending into two measures, and, in any case, the second ending does not have the same number of measures as the first ending. It seems best to call the first measure of the first ending 34a, and the next measure 34a' (followed, if necessary, by 34a''). Then the single measure of the second ending is 34b. Measure 35 is the one that begins with a d-minor arpeggio in the bass.

Now that we have examined full sonata movements, our remaining studies will once again focus on smaller subjects. This apparent regression actually represents a step forward, for the final chapters will investigate more difficult, even somewhat experimental, tonal music. The reduced size of the compositions will facilitate the more detailed approach required in a consideration of more highly developed tonal music. We will find that even the identification of items in progression may be a difficult task; and yet such identifications must be made before relationships, connections, and developments can be noticed.

As usual, the surface characteristics of the music will provide an orientation. This brief composition of Brahms, like most small pieces, seems to present one unified surface; unlike the sonata movements, it does not seem to be populated by a variety of contrasting themes and motives. But, on closer inspection, we find that simple contrasts and identifications exist. The fairly consistent eighth-note motion that seems to characterize the piece does not actually appear until measure 8; the music up to the downbeat of measure 8 is slower and more ponderous. Similarly, the faster music does not last until the end, but ceases in measure 37, giving way once more to less active music in measure 38. When we next notice that the slower music at the end—the final eight measures —duplicates that at the beginning, a clear A–B–A shape emerges. Perhaps the piece seems a little misshapen this way, with the B section so bloated that it seems to consume the entire composition; since the middle section begins so soon after the music starts, we may tend not to regard measure 8 as a fundamental slicing point, and thus lose our sense of orientation. But the unique downbeat octave in that measure, combined with the first (admittedly brief) complete silence, cannot easily be overlooked; and the weighty two beats' silence that punctuates the second division, at measure 38, is a further indication of form. Deeper analytic investigation will strengthen this impression of the shape of the piece.

Beginning with the A section, we find that it neatly divides into phrase statements separated or connected by solo or octave-doubled "filler." The first of these statements occupies the first five beats, through beat 3 of the first full measure.[1] Before focusing on the content of this opening unit, we can note its relation to the remaining utterances of the A section: the second phrase appears as an echo to the first (it is softer and reduced in registral spread, while presenting the same melody with a slightly altered harmony), and the third resembles the first more closely, while expanding it greatly. We will see how the unfinished business of the first unit is prolonged by the second and then resolved by the third, and how the effects of "echo" (reduction) and expansion, respectively, project these functions of the units in this scheme.

All lines of the initial statement follow paths that describe intervals of the a-minor (tonic) triad (Ex. 10–1). The soprano line, doubled an octave lower, presents the triad interval E–A, first as a direct skip, and then filled in by scalar passing tones. The bass line, similarly doubled in octaves, moves through the a-minor interval A–C, by way of the passing tone B. Meanwhile, the only other line, just beneath the melody, simply

---

1. Though the music is notated in cut time, a four-beat conception of the measures is convenient for locating points in time.

Ex. 10-1

prolongs the tonic-triad pitch C, with the neighbor embellishment C–C–D–C.

The alignment into chords of these tonic-triad-produced lines, however, is curious. Of course they meet to form an a-minor triad at the first attack. But as they find their way back into the tonic triad, no line actually strikes the pitch A; the final chord of the unit is made up of C's and E's—notes of the tonic triad, to be sure, but presented more to suggest the C triad. The ratio of C's to E's, combined with the unfilled C octave in the bass, clearly weights the chord in favor of the C triad. Following the bass line, then, we hear it moving through an interval of the a-minor triad, but at its conclusion (resolution) we reinterpret its last pitch as a member of a different triad (C). More surprising, with the other lines we find ourselves following paths that end up reinterpreting the initial pitch (E or C, depending on the line) in a new context.

In the middle of these two stations (the initial a and the final C) the lines meet to form a G triad. Then the upper line moves to F while the other lines sustain D and B, resulting in a dominant-seventh inflection of the G chord, which then moves quite properly to C.

The result of these various effects is a movement in tonic focus from A to C over the course of the first brief phrase. Of course the a-minor context is capable of embracing both centers, since it contains both pitch classes (A and C), and the movement from one to the other can be thought of as projecting the tonic-triad interval A–C. But we should note the role the peculiar metrical situation plays in our confrontation with these notes, for Brahms frequently tampers with meter. In this case, though the phrase would seem to fit perfectly well into the usual four-beat bar pattern, with the initial and final poles (the a and C triads) stressed on the two downbeats, the unit is "shifted back" two beats. The only item to receive downbeat stress is, curiously enough, the G chord; so neither station receives direct preference, but perhaps a slight edge toward the focus of C is implied, since the G chord is heard in terms of the C chord to which it moves, and which it helps tonicize.

At the end of this first, meaningful statement the pitch E emerges from its thick surroundings, and forms the connecting link between the two (related) first phrases. (The D♯, clearly subordinated by its rhythm, functions throughout as a neighbor to E.) E would seem to be a very appropriate connector, since it is shared by both the a and the C triads, but is, significantly (unlike the pitches A and C), tonic of neither. Thus, as it sounds alone between the two phrases, it seems to straddle the a–C world, balancing the two tonalities that have been bridged by the first phrase; we are poised between phrases, but also between two triadic worlds, between which we cannot yet choose.

The ambiguity of the connecting E is most effective at the start of the second (repeat) phrase, on the third beat of measure 2. For here we don't know whether to think of the E in terms of the a triad—the way we would expect the first melody note of the repetition to be harmonized —or the C triad, the last-reached harmony. (In fact, for a moment we don't even know whether E is to be heard as the start of a repetition phrase or just another in the series of filler E's; of course, it is both.) The form of the echo-repetition prolongs and even deepens the confusion. For with the E unharmonized, the A harmonized now with an F triad, and the G chord presented in root position, the phrase now reads out clearly in C, with a IV–V–I cadence into the C chord that ends this second statement.

It is curious to note that the F chord has been carefully prepared for. The second beat of the *first* phrase consists just of A–C, which at that point we have no reason to interpret in any way other than a minor. But this interval is just as well part of the F triad, which then occupies this second-beat slot in the *repeat* phrase. So the intervals of the original a triad seem to generate these new harmonies by reinterpretation (Ex. 10–2). The a-minor triad quickly "exhausts" its thirds, giving them over to new triads; in so doing, it relinquishes its position as tonic to C, which, incidentally, is the one shared pitch element.

We can read out the lines of this second phrase in terms of the C triad, even though the melody is the same as it was in the a-triad–governed

Ex. 10-2

```
                    G

             E·······E

     C·······C·······C

       A····· A

       F
      ◄────·───►
```

first phrase. The bass line, F–G–C, describes an interval of the C triad
(G–C), embellishing the triadic G with an incomplete lower neighbor
(F). The tenor line simply moves within the C triad (E–C–G–G). The
alto line describes the triad interval E–C, embellishing the C with a
neighbor formation. And the melody can be interpreted with A as incomplete neighbor to the now-triadic G (an interpretation suggested
by the rhythm, which now works clearly to stress the G on the downbeat
of measure 3); the melody then works within the C-triad interval E–G
(Ex. 10–3).

Ex. 10-3

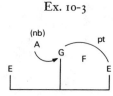

Once again E emerges to play its connecting role, and leads now to
the third, final and extended statement of this motivic unit. The extension
of this closing version serves to turn the tonic focus back to A, which is
most clearly articulated by the completely empty quadruple octave on
the downbeat of measure 8, where all motion ceases.

The phrase starts out (third beat of measure 4) with the same E
ambiguity; if anything, we are inclined to hear the E as a member of
the C triad. But on the second beat of the phrase the A is harmonized
with a root-position (and root-quadrupled!) a-minor chord, and we can
interpret the melodic interval E–A, the first interval of the phrase, once
again in the a triad (as in the first instance of the phrase, and as opposed to
the middle phrase, where the status of the interval was in question).

The phrase now moves as it did originally, toward C (with the bass
moving up to C, the melody moving down to E). But the arrival of C

is obscured by a new rhythmic feature: the staggering of the voices provides for a complete C statement only on the last half of the last beat of measure 5; most of that C chord is then heard out of place, over the bass D that enters on the next downbeat.

Indeed this time C is not a goal, but is just passed through. For the phrase now carries the melody to B and the bass to E, presenting an E triad that serves as dominant of a. This is the first dominant for a we have had, and the G♯ is the first leading tone to A in the music. These facts are striking tokens of the severe and carefully wrought ambiguity the composer has set up as a structure for this opening section.

With the arrival of this dominant, the phrase splits into two sub-phrases. Significantly, the gap is bridged in the bass by the same E–D♯–E connecting detail that has bridged all previous phrase separations. This time, however, the function of the E is absolutely clear: it is the dominant pitch, and it moves directly into A by way of C, thus outlining the entire a-minor triad.

Meanwhile, over the course of this third phrase, the melody has traced a simple descending a-minor scale, which reaches the second degree by the end of the first part of the third phrase. After the separation, then, the scale is completed by way of a slight retracing, which presents the bottom third of the triad, C–A, filled in with B. (Simultaneously the bass connects its repeated "filler," E, to C; thus both thirds of the a-minor triad are arpeggiated at this point. These two phrases end at just the same time, and then both voices move directly to the declarative A octave, which finalizes the reestablishment of a minor that these voices have just been projecting.) The final melodic C–B–A perhaps balances the initial bass A–B–C. Together these two polar details summarize the essential harmonic action of the A section, the move from a to C and back (thus, of course, projecting the interval A–C of the tonic triad). The dynamics help present this overall picture: the initial a minor is marked *mp,* which softens to *p* by the time C has been established but then goes back to *mp* when a minor is reintroduced. Even the metrical situation is involved in this picture. (We have already noted its initial contribution to the focal ambiguity, but, in fact, we find *throughout* the phrase a kind of rhythmic parallel to the uncertain pitch focus: is the first beat or the third beat of each measure the "referential" one?) Perhaps the first time the downbeat is straightened out is in measure 8, where the ensuing motion clarifies the metrical positioning of the notes. So this comes about just when the a-minor focus is permanently installed at the end of the first section.

Finally, we can note the overall melodic plan that rests on this curious harmonic foundation. For the descending a scale seen from the end of measure 4 to the end of the section actually seems more like the continuation (and ultimate completion) of an attempted a-minor scalar descent begun before the first measure. Thus, in the sense that the third phrase carries a previously begun project to its conclusion, our view of the third phrase as an extension of the first is borne out. In an even more fundamental sense, however, this A to A descent may seem to be embedded in a five-note descent from the first E; for the form of the motive is to insert the descending fourth between two polar E's, which perhaps then get prolonged by the later such E's in measures 4 and 5, finally to descend into the tonic at the end of the section (Ex. 10–4). This overall melodic

Ex. 10-4

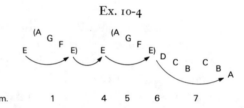

descent from E can then be matched with the underlying harmonic action, with the result that we can see the way E is prolonged long enough to be reinterpreted in C and then again in a before it descends (Ex. 10–5).

Ex. 10-5

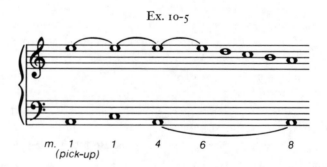

This section, then, is cleanly separated from the middle section, which separates this music from its literal repeat at the end of the piece. Even a cursory familiarity with the B section reveals its fundamental connection to the surrounding A sections, and ultimately its function in the piece. For the middle section begins just with the alternations of E and D♯ already so prominent in section A. (Perhaps the reappearance of these notes in the bass at the end of section A is a way of linking the earlier, more pronounced presence of the figure to its new prominence here.) And as we begin to listen through the middle section, we discover that this figure is not just the entrance into the section, but the very theme of it: it reappears immediately in measure 10, and then repeatedly in measures 12, 13, and 14; thereafter transpositions of this figure carry the music along through the end of the section. Thus we see that the middle section, whose function, after all, is really to connect two statements of the A section, is made out of a figure (E–D♯ alternations) that originally served precisely that function *within* the A section—to connect statements of the A section theme. The linking *particle* in the first two measures of the piece has exploded into a whole linking *section*.

Furthermore, the entire rhythmic format of the piece projects this relationship. We first noticed that the middle section is characterized by eighth-note music, in contrast to the slower outer-section music. But the eighth-note motion itself has its origin in the connecting detail, E–D♯–E, in measure 1 (where the single eighth-note detail grows smoothly out of the rhythmicization of the F passing tone of which the E–D♯ figure is a distinct echo as well as an intervallic mirror!).

Such a secure understanding of the middle section in its general and essential workings is a necessary background for more detailed study of the music, for the middle section is devious and challenging. We will begin slowly, with a consideration of some initial linear details.

The section opens by connecting our E–D♯ figure to C. This is immediately apprehensible, however, in several ways: first, the interval so described is one of the a-minor triad, just firmly established (as well as of the C-major triad, just put aside); second, the immediately previous instance of the E–D♯ detail, in the bass of measures 6–7, similarly joins these notes to C (explicitly, with a phrasing indication); finally, we can discover that even the first appearance of this detail shows the concluding E moving directly to C (last beat of measure 2, middle voices). We may now want to learn to hear the opening passage in terms of this new detail, which only becomes apparent in the solo line in measure 8.

But the slur in measure 8 lasts longer, proceeding one note further to G♯. As a shape, of course, this just imitates the previous bass shape (which moves to A after the C). But in moving to G♯, this new line describes neither the a-minor triad nor the C-major triad. Rather, it seems to straddle the two, with G♯ poised just midway between A, which would complete an a triad, and G, which would form a C triad (Ex. 10–6). Harmonically the sonority projects the ambiguity by forming an augmented triad type, with both thirds equal in size, and no pitch asserting a root quality.

Ex. 10-6

E D# E C
A ?
E D# E C
G#
E D# E C
G ?

Intriguing as these speculations may be, we still need a function for G♯ in a normal grammatical context. This context is clearly supplied by all the other notes in the first half of measure 9. For G♯ moves directly to A, which then links with C to present an a-minor interval, and the whole is accompanied by a simple a-minor arpeggiation in the bass. The only trouble is rhythmic: G♯ is long and on a downbeat, A (to which G♯ presumably refers, as lower neighbor) is short and not even *on* any beat. This is one of the predominant rhythmic (and, hence, pitch) features of the middle section, and, if properly understood, it will clear the way for easier interpretation of harmonic and linear details. In large part this condition accounts for much of the difficulty of this kind of music, because, with so much relative attention paid to the nontriadic elements, the notion of reference—on which all our tonal understanding has been based—becomes partially obscured.[2]

This property is immediately manifest in the next melodic detail. In a linear sense, the E in measure 10 must be the reference for the D♯ in measure 9, which is its neighbor. Once again, the D♯ is long and emphasized, the more important E very temporary. At the same time this new detail continues to invoke the E–D♯ figure, and in fact restores it to its original register (from measure 1), while rounding out the first phrase

2. If ever the referential connections became totally obscured by such weightings, the sense in which the music would be "tonal" would be highly questionable. This is, in one sense, just what transpired historically as the tonal system aged. See the Conclusion.

of section B with the same notes with which it begins.[3] (The eighth notes at the end of measure 10 clearly begin a new phrase by imitating the opening of the section.)

This last D♯–E pair, over the measure 9–10 bar line, introduces the next phrase with an octave coupling of the E (thus making even more explicit the connection between the beginning and ending of the phrase, both with E–D♯'s). The next phrase presents again the figure leading to G♯, and again the G♯ seems to be resolved by the brief A in measure 11; but this time the continuation of the phrase seems to keep G♯ alive (downbeat of measure 12). In fact, with an acceleration of the G♯-ending figure, this pitch is prolonged until, surprisingly, it resolves not to A (as it repeatedly does locally now) but, ultimately, down to G (measure 15, at the bottom of the treble chords, which at first come about simply by retention from the motive at the end of measure 14). Notice the re-spelling of G♯ as A♭ on the downbeat of measure 15.

We now see that the original ambiguity of the G♯ of measure 9, poised between A and G, has produced the meaning of the whole first part of the B section (which apparently splits at the repeat sign). For if G♯ resolves to A, we are still in a minor; if it resolves to G, we are back in C major! This is just what happens over the course of this first part of the middle section, and we have seen this accomplished as yet only linearly in the treble.

3. It is interesting to return to the original version of E–D♯ to follow a progression that further justifies the figure in measure 8. Note the three configurations in the accompanying example, already related by the common move from E to C.

What makes the progression particularly interesting to learn to hear (besides its giving us a new way to understand the augmented triad figure that opens the new section) is that each step in the progression takes place in a different register, and these positions fan out, an octave in each direction, from the original central one. The figure in measure 2, that is, is moved down an octave for measure 7, up an octave for measure 8. Even more interesting is the fact that the original position in measure 2 is actually a *contraction* of this registral spread, first introduced in the opening phrase! The connection between the gradual spreading out (through this progression) and the original contraction is quite close, for the bass figure in measures 7–8 dips down to the low A, which is the low note of the opening chord, while the figure in measure 8 centers around the E, which is the top note of the opening chord. So these figures expand back to the points from which the original figure in the progression has contracted!

But the harmony clearly follows just this path, from a minor to C. The first two phrases (measures 9–12) present simple i to V connections, each time by way of the embellishing diminished-seventh chord, which acts both as a dominant type to E (like a B⁷, that is) and as a linking stack of neighbors to the a-minor chord on the left and the V chord on the right. In each case the lines, while performing their noted linear jobs, fit in equally well. (For example, above the a-minor bass arpeggiation in measure 9, the G♯ acts as lower neighbor to the A, to which it moves before the chord has finished. Meanwhile, the melodic A, C, and D♯ spell out the diminished seventh linearly; and the E, to which the D♯ resolves, is part of the V chord.)

After the V chord in measure 12, the harmony clearly and simply reads out in C. The F chord in measure 13 acts as a subdominant, moving to the V/V in measure 14, to the C⁶₄, and then through V⁷ into I (C, the downbeat of measure 16a). In fact, reading the bass line of the bass part (the succession of lowest notes, which are also downbeats), we now find a clear delineation of the C-major triad: we start with E on the downbeat of measure 12 (choosing this starting point because, with reference to *either* the a or C triad, the previous low D♯ is, once again, a neighbor, and we start hearing a motion with its resolution in E), pass chromatically through F and F♯ (the next two downbeats) into G (downbeat of measure 15), which is appropriately repeated, and thence to C. The motion thus delineates E–G–C, following the C-major triad.

The treble chords toward the end of this first part of section B follow the same path into C. The final motivic figure in the series, in measure 14, features a retention of its notes into the augmented triad (downbeat of measure 15), which duplicates the one that initiated the whole section (measures 8–9, treble). It is followed by a G⁷ chord, which is then altered by the chromatic motion of the D♯ (chromatic passing tone from D to E), and finally resolves in the C chord in measure 16a. The top note of the resolving chord is E, which leads the way to a repetition of the whole section—that is, right back into a minor, for a repeat performance of the journey into C.

The overall accomplishment of this part of the music, then, is just a grand expansion of the accomplishment of the very first (generating) phrase: to bring the harmonic focus from A to C, thus moving through an interval of the tonic triad. With this as background, the composer weaves a web of motivic detail. The entire section has proceeded according to the E–C motive of measure 8 (itself derived, as demonstrated, from the "filler" material of the A section), which projects an interval of both the a-minor and C-major polar triads. More locally generated details, such as the following, should be studied: the G♯–A–C melodic segment in measure 9 is echoed in the bass as the succession of lowest notes (C–A–G♯). The next bass succession of the same sort, C–D♯–E (beginning in measure 11), just echoes the melodic continuation (C–D♯–E, measures 9–10, starting where the last echoed melodic segment leaves off). It is interesting to note that these two figures are inversions of each other (Ex. 10–7), and that the second version obviously can generate the E–D♯–E–C figure that dominates the music.

Ex. 10-7

The repetition of measures 9–16 now takes place, hinging on the E–D♯–E–C motive in measure 16a, which explicitly doubles as an item of the newly established C triad and of the a-minor triad arriving over the (repeat) bar line. After that the continuation of the B section is fairly easy to follow. Since in measure 24 a general repeat of the music from measure 9 seems to begin, we can regard the music between these areas (that is, measures 17–23) as a connecting unit between the two fundamental, outer areas of B. And so the middle section itself has an a–b–a form that is a reduction of the form of the whole piece.

Further study of the B section, of which we will only present some highlighting details, will confirm that this shape for the middle section continues to project the a–C dichotomy. The center area of the B section (measures 17–23) serves to prolong the C tonality that is the consequence of the first part of the section. Then the last part of the B section, starting in measure 24, returns to a minor and works its way back to C (in the first ending, thus connecting once again to measure 17, the C prolongation area) or, alternatively, back to a minor (the second ending) in preparation for the final statement (in a) of the opening music. Thus the overall tonal form of the middle section (Ex. 10–8) is, like the A section, a large-scale projection of the tonic-triad interval A–C; and by turning toward C and then returning to a over

Ex. 10-8

m. 9-16 ("a")   m. 17-23 ("b")   m. 24-37 ("a")

a → C :‖:   C   a

the course of the section, it just expands on the job done so much more
succinctly in the A section, which similarly moves from a to C and back.
Ex. 10–9 shows how the entire composition, viewed harmonically "from
the air," might appear.

Ex. 10-9

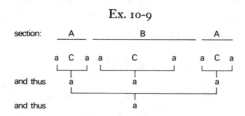

section: A   B   A

             a C a a   C   a   a C a

and thus   a   a   a

and thus   a

Furthermore, we can, because of the persistence of the E-expressing
motive throughout the middle section, fit an overall melodic journey
onto this harmonic picture—a journey which, like that harmonic picture,
serves just to project the tonic triad. For if we take the prominence of
the fourth-space treble E in the middle section as an indication that the
substantial E in section A only descends to its A *locally* (see example
10–5), but is otherwise prolonged by the use of the motive, then we can
regard the repetition of the A section at the end of the piece as the true
and permanent descent (Ex. 10–10). The harmonic games that are played

Ex. 10-10

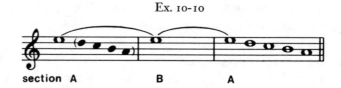

section A   B   A

under this suspended E (its continual reinterpretation, on all levels, al-
ternately as a member of the a triad and of the C triad) constitute the
bulk of the composition (Ex. 10–11).

The remainder of the B section should provide ample opportunity for
continued study of complex tonal relations. As always, identification
of materials should precede any higher-level drawing of relations and

Ex. 10-11

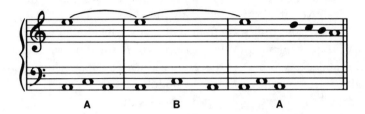

patterns (since the general survey of that stretch of the music has already been accomplished).

A few details may point the way. The music starting in measure 17 precedes the locally prominent C triad by a chain of dominant types (essentially A^7–D^7–G^7–C or familiar dissonant variants of these), which, once again, span the A to C gap, thus presenting at an even more local level the same A–C connection seen at all higher (broader) levels. With the extreme outer voices switched, this unit is repeated directly in the following two measures (19–20). These two statements constitute the principal matter of the "C"-oriented middle area of the middle section. (Note that here we connect not A, or a, to C, but a dissonant A-meaning chord, the A^7 on the downbeat of measure 17; so C clearly predominates, and is, in fact, the only real triad in the area, the D chord being in the dissonant $^6_4$ position.)

The lengthened $^3_2$ measure (23) may feel like a significant lingering just prior to a switch in tonal focus (from C to a). The stretching in the first ending later on seems to function the same way, and at a comparable point (the tonic focus again about to switch, from a to C; notice in comparison that the *second* ending seems more *compact*, with the a-minor tonality, arrived at a few measures earlier, *not* about to change, but installed now for the rest of the piece). The F♯ that is a thorn in the otherwise pure (and purely presented—see the bass and then the last treble chord) a-minor complex of measures 21–22 turns out to be a protracted upper neighbor to the very important E of measure 24; its reappearance in a more suitable context as part of the B^7 (dominant to E) in measure 23 suggests the anticipatory nature of its dissonant appearance in measure 21.

The reappearance of rhythmic and metrical irregularities after the second ending (starting in measure 35) foreshadows the return of the principal A section, with its constant metrical ambiguity. The obscuring of the beat by heavy syncopation in the first ending, just as in measures 21–22, is apparently associated with the abrupt shift in tonality about to take place (and thus this effect is absent in the second ending, where no such shift is imminent). In measures 36–37 the unusual alignment of pitches and beats prevents the establishment of a convincing a-minor cadence to resolve the issues of the middle section—a role filled by (reserved for) the repeating A section itself as a unit.

Additionally, pitch and pitch-rhythm alignment irregularities abound, and the reader is referred especially to aspects of measures 24, 30, 35, and 36, in addition to other spots already brought briefly to the reader's attention.

A Study of the
End of Act I of
Wagner's *Die Walküre*

We now take a more drastic step in reducing the size of the pieces chosen for study, by returning to the analysis of a fragment. But we could hardly choose otherwise if we wish to study some music by a composer who figured so prominently and crucially in the final stages of development of the tonal system, for Wagner's compositions are extremely large. The fifty-five-measure fragment reproduced in Ex. 11–1 is an excerpt from *Der Ring des Nibelungen*. The four lengthy operas that constitute the cycle were conceived of by the composer (and are apparently perceived by many listeners) as forming the primary slices of a single piece. The first and briefest of these operas, *Das Rheingold*, lasts over two hours and features completely continuous music from start to finish. The next smallest slices, then, are the complete acts of the remaining operas; these acts, though divided into scenes, are also each musically continuous. And so, at the *smallest*, we have, separated by silence, chunks of continuous music, none of which is less than an hour in duration (and most are impressively longer). And with such large units presenting themselves as the smallest candidates for "piecehood," we can hardly, as with our multimovement sonatas, hope to approach an entire such "movement" analytically.

Since we are dealing, then, with a fragment, we must once again

Ex. 11-1

Ex. 11–1 (*continued*)

Ex. 11–1 (*continued*)

remind ourselves of the limits we should expect to place on our goals. We cannot seek an overall shape or progression, or expect to witness the completion of long-range compositional objectives. In this sense, we will be "studying" rather than "analyzing."

Other instructive problems will arise. On becoming familiar with Wagner's later music, we discover that chordal items match the pure triad model of vertical sonority less often than in the tonal music we have been studying. The same condition holds for the linear formations, which follow the triad less clearly (if at all). And while these features do not make the *Ring* operas nearly as tonally confusing as *Tristan und Isolde*, we can expect to encounter some of this difficulty here.

Wagner's very special and unique use of time and his sense of temporal unfolding of pitch structures is likely to cause analytic confusion at first. For in these huge pieces time often moves very slowly, with events sometimes taking place very gradually. In some passages a whole phrase, or even a whole page of phrases, accomplishes no more than what would be handled by a single chordal attack in other tonal music. So our sense of range in this music may be confused or distorted; what may appear as the long or middle range may actually be, here, the short range (local); and the short range may appear unusually static.

Another challenge to the analyst, one that is actually related to the problem of time, is the system of motivic units—those famous "leit-motifs," whose ostensible purpose is the identification of a character, object, idea, or other such literal element of the story. From a purely musical point of view, it is clear that Wagner uses these motives to expand the size of a musical event. One motive, for example, may be a brief tune that is always accompanied by some applied dominant–tonic motion; it may then be invoked to express or prolong a given V–I motion. Even more simply, many of these motives are just particular arpeggiated forms of what would otherwise be a succinct and solitary triad statement. We will find clear examples of this idea in the excerpt under study.

So interesting are all these "problems" that the question "Why bother to study Wagner?" can hardly arise. Like Brahms, Wagner was an experimenter; his music, therefore, cannot fail to show us new possibilities inherent in the properties of the remarkable tonal system.

The choice of fragment here depends, again, on the special characteristics of Wagner's music. An entire act is very extensive, musical issues develop very slowly, and the fabric is strictly continuous. We choose, then, to slice a portion from the very *end* of an act; there, at least, something may be seen to happen. And, in fact, we can start with the final cadence that brings with it the curtain to Act I of *Die Walküre*.

Clearly enough, the ultimate event in the act is a root-position G-major triad. Strangely, though, this final chord is not on the downbeat of the last measure, but on the weaker second beat. And though it must be nearly impossible to project this sense of weakness physically (considering the dynamics as well as the time elapsing since the previous attack), we can still imagine that the composer is trying to convey something unusual about this final chord.

The weakened condition of the last attack is only the last in a series of strange impairments. Reading backwards into the opera, we next discover that this final tonic chord is preceded not by a standard dominant or dominant-seventh chord, but by the more dissonant dominant-related diminished seventh. Certainly this chord performs the same kind of function as the true dominant, and contains the important linear connections into the tonic pitch from leading tone and second degree; but the lack of V–I root movement in the bass seems to impair the sense of strong arrival at the tonic, which we know now will be further weakened by its metrical placement. Furthermore, the diminished seventh is placed over a G pedal, which has a double effect: the chord is made even more dissonant (with the addition of more dissonant intervals), and the sense of movement *from* a dominant type *to* a tonic is reduced by the unifying and embracing action of the bass G.

Rhythmic problems join the problematical pitch situation to create an even stranger effect. In contrast to the final chord, the penultimate chord *is* squarely on the downbeat, is the first chord marked *fff*, and lasts fully nine times longer than the chord to which it presumably resolves. (If the G chord were on a downbeat, it would generate a sense of "lasting" for the entire measure or for a group of measures—even if it were notated to last just one beat. Such an effect is harder to imagine with the chord coming on the offbeat.) Perhaps we can focus on the total effect here by trying to picture the motion of the melodic A into the G in terms of a typical, ultimate passing of the second degree down into the final tonic pitch. Compared thus with all the other tonal endings we have studied, the peculiarities of this cadence may strike with greater force. There may even be a sense in which we can feel that this A is left unresolved at the conclusion of the act!

As we penetrate a little further back into the music, we do, however, find the makings of a clear V⁷–I statement for G. The downbeat of the fifth-to-last measure (marked *ff*) seems to be the resolution of the D⁷ chord that is unambiguously displayed in the bass part of the previous two measures; above this bass V⁷ the treble seems to move chromatically up from D (accented, at *più f*) to what must surely be expected to be G (at the point where the V⁷ resolves). But here again, on this downbeat, another strange interruption occurs (Ex. 11–2). The resolving G chord is

Ex. 11-2

shockingly topped by a (doubled) A, a second degree that apparently is a stand-in for the expected G. (Thus the leading tone F♯, from the previous measure, skips up rather than steps, overshooting the tonic pitch.) Above the otherwise untroubled G chord this A persists for a full measure, after which we surely expect its firm resolution to the first degree. But once again the resolution is deeply troubled; for the A merely slips into the G on the offbeat (in the fourth-to-last measure) and weakly slides down a G arpeggiation, only to land squarely on the last, long, dissonant A first discussed.

We see, then, that the act does close with a V–I cadence in G, but one thickly studded with delaying, diverting, and distorting details. In order to slice off an ending to the act that concludes this way, it seems fair to look back as far as the next-previous root position G chord. Incredibly enough, we must look back a full fifty-five measures to find such a chord; and we have numbered our measures, from 1 to 55, from that point. Between these two points, to be sure, many G-major items are present; most, however, are in the dissonant ⁶₄ position, and all others contain detracting elements (like the A in measure 51). In contrast, measure "1" is a pure, root-position tonic chord, properly spaced and balanced, lasting the entire measure. It seems like a convenient place to start.

A brief survey of the territory bounded by these unique root-position G chords produces a simple map to guide us through. The tenor (identified as "Siegm." in the score) sings until the downbeat of measure 9; the soprano (indicated as "Siegl.") takes over, finishing on the downbeat of measure 20; the tenor resumes, and sings until the downbeat of measure 30; the orchestra then plays alone until the end of the act. We can refer to these sections as A, B, C, D (measures 1–9, 9–20, 20–30, 30–55, with the downbeats forming the dividing points), especially since tempo changes are associated with these precise slicing points (between A and B and between B and C; then section D is even more clearly demarcated by the absence of singing).

Three of these four sections end with some kind of important G. On the downbeat of measure 9 the tenor ends his line with G; since the tempo changes at that point, the G forms the link between the two sections, as last pitch of A and first pitch of B. Similarly between sections B and C, G is the linking pitch, being the final note of the vocal line there (and thus, it turns out, the last soprano note in the act). And, of course, the end of section D, the end of the music altogether, is the G cadence as described.

The section C–D division is marked by another significant musical formation, a clear dominant–tonic arrival—but not in G. The nature and place of this cadence we will consider in turn. We will start with the contents and accomplishments of the A phrase first.

The first phrase is infused with a motive—one of these melodic fragments that becomes standardized over the course of the entire work, making its appearance in predictable dramatic environments, but also conveying a fairly unchanging *musical* message (Ex. 11–3). In this case

Ex. 11-3

the fragment usually brings with it a dominant–tonic motion, with (in this particular transposition) the D♯ acting as chromatic passing tone between the D and E, which form the (inverted) seventh of the E^7 chord; the next two notes, B and D, continue the E^7 arpeggiation, while the final note, C, represents the resolution of the entire chord into a minor; usually the D is heard as an appoggiatura to the C, with the harmony changing (resolving) on the downbeat.

In this passage (measures 2–3) the "E^7–a" context of the motive is perfectly clear. With E as the next pitch to follow (end of measure 3, bass staff), the a-minor interval C–E is produced within the established a-minor context, and the resulting E is suspended to introduce a transposition of the motive a major second higher, which thus accomplishes the move $F\sharp^7$–b (measures 4–5). Notice, meanwhile, that the pitch E is common to all of these chords but the last (E^7, a, $F\sharp^7$), and hence is sustained throughout in the vocal part, long enough to double the motive E (downbeat of measure 5) and resolve, with that motive pitch, to D (on the syllable "-mund").

A context for this activity is soon provided. The b-minor resolution in measure 5 quickly turns into a diminished seventh, which acts as a dominant type for a minor, thus completing an a-minor segment on the downbeat of measure 6 (Ex. 11–4). But this a-minor situation is

Ex. 11-4

m. 2-3   m. 6

E^7-a   a

surrounded exactly by two bordering G chords, the one that begins the passage (measure 1), and the one that immediately follows (in the $^6_4$ position: measure 7). G in fact provides the overall context for the phrase, with the E^7 in measure 2 growing out of G by way of the shared interval B–D, and the entire a-minor area functioning as ii. With the return of the $^6_4$ G in measure 7 we should be ready for a G cadence; for $^6_4$ is followed by a standard root-position V^7 (D, measure 8), just as the voice reaches the second-degree A.

The entire phrase begins to take shape. The long-sustained E in the voice part is just an accented upper neighbor to the G-triadic D of measures 1 and 5, which then begins a descent (through C, B, and A) to the tonic G, which is actually reached on the downbeat of measure 9, at the point where we have sliced the music in our initial survey.

It is just at this point that the first of a series of disappointments, cul-
minating in the complicated final cadence, occurs. For though the melodic A resolves directly into G, it is completely misharmonized, and thus
is not given a chance to sound in any real sense resolved. At first, squarely
on the downbeat of measure 9, the resolution seems like a standard V–vi
deceptive cadence, for the downbeat chord, for three-quarters of a beat,
appears just as E–G, suggesting the e-minor triad. The appearance of C♯
in the orchestral treble at the end of the first beat confuses the identity
of the resolution chord. We can discover the contents of this chord by
following its gradual development over the course of five measures
in the bass; first C♯ gets added (measure 10, as already suggested by the
melodic C♯ in measure 9), and then B (end of measure 12). The chord is
then complete, as the bass orchestral anticipation figure announces over
the 12–13 bar line (Ex. 11–5). With this information we can read out the

Ex. 11-5

entire first six measures of the B area. The orchestral bass, of course, just
develops this chord. The orchestral treble presents a series of three-note
units whose first and last notes are always of this E–G–B–C♯ complex;
in each case, then, the middle pitch can be interpreted as an accented
neighbor (always a half step away) to the third (chordal) pitch. And the
vocal part just skips around among the pitches of the chord, with the
single exception of the D on the downbeat of measure 12, which (if we
give an interpretation that parallels the reading of the orchestral treble
music) acts as an accented upper neighbor to C♯. The orchestra ends the
slow unfolding of this chord by arpeggiating quickly and unambiguously
through it (the sixteenths in measure 13). We see here, then, an example
of Wagner's special treatment of time. This "resolving" chord, E–G–
B–C♯, is not just stated as a downbeat attack, but is used to generate an
entire phrase (harmony as well as melody). The phrase then takes the
place of the single attack.

This "single attack" has been identified as the G substitute for the
resolution of the D[7] that ends the A phrase. The first half of the B phrase,
then, just plays out this "wrong turn." The curious resolving chord might

sound like an e-minor chord with an added sixth (C♯); the use of E in
the bass projects this view, as well as the familiar V–vi pattern to which
D⁷–e would conform. Here we might also be drawing upon the long-
sustained vocal E in the A phrase as preparation.

On the "right" side, however, we might want to focus on the A⁷
aspects of this E–G–B–C♯ chord (that is, C♯–E–G); for on this end of
the situation the chord does move directly to D⁷ (from which it arose),
on the downbeat of measure 15. Just as this D⁷ may remind us where
we originally have been (G), the next chord, B⁷ (sharing A–F♯ with the
previous chord), invokes e minor once again! A struggle between e and
G is becoming apparent. The long E in measures 3–5 takes on added
significance: in assuming more emphasis than the D to which it locally
resolves, it sets up the whole e–G dichotomy (D being, of course, a
representative of the G tonality). Note further that the voice part in the
beginning of the B phrase outlines the e triad, but the pitch G struggles
to the fore (measures 13–14).

When next B⁷ moves to C on the downbeat of measure 16, the e–G
controversy takes a new turn. For in e this motion can be a V–VI deceptive cadence; but C is also the subdominant of G, and it acts so here. The
voice part finally projects E as, again, the upper neighbor to D (measure
19), and the voice works its way to another landing squarely on G (measure 20, the end of the phrase).

But the point is, this arrival is just another in the series of frustrations.
For though the harmony works its way clearly toward G (the subdominant moves to G⁶₄ by way of the connecting diminished seventh
in measure 17; the G⁶₄ then proceeds in standard fashion to the V⁷ in
measure 19, ready to resolve to G along with the voice), the final cadence
is once again avoided. In place of a G chord on the downbeat of measure
20 we are presented with the sonority E–G–B♭–D. Perhaps we can understand this chord as growing out of the earlier G substitution by way of
the diminished seventh in measure 17 (Ex. 11–6). On the outgoing side,

Ex. 11-6

C# ——	C#	D
B	B♭ ——	B♭
G ——	G ——	G
E ——	E ——	E
m. 9-14	17	20

however, this chord just looks like a stack of neighbors to the A⁷ chord
that follows it (and this relation is borne out as the C phrase unfolds)
(Ex. 11–7).

Ex. 11-7

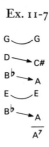

So far the A and B phrases seem to be approaching the same goal in
different ways. In both cases the music works its way to what seems to
be a G cadence, complete with I_4^6 and V⁷ in clear succession. In both
cases, also, the resolving vocal pitch, each time associated with a major
phrase division, is actually G. But both times the cadence is frustrated
by the appearance of unexpected material in place of the final G chord.

In these terms, phrase C is even more astonishing. At the conclusion
of that phrase the voices have finished their contribution to the act. Appropriately, they do so with a cadence. The problem is, this cadence is
not in G. That is, the vocal music does not end in the key that the act
itself clearly ends in, and that has been implied for the past two phrases.

This surprising turn of events is linked to the foregoing in the most
interesting ways. First of all, the cadential key here (measure 30) is e
minor. This is unambiguously displayed by all forces from measure 27 to
the cadence in measure 30: e_3^5 climbs to e_4^6 by lines that describe e intervals; a B⁷ then supplies all the usual dominant-seventh effects for the final
root-position e chord. Now this key is just the alternative that has been
involved, in various ways and on various levels, all along. We can now
go back and make new sense out of all the E-related items, whose significance in the previous two phrases could not be guessed earlier. The
long-sustained melodic E in phrase A, which nearly outweighed the D
to which it resolved; the e-containing cadence chord that ends A and
forms so much of the B phrase; the clear delineation of the e triad by the
voice in measures 10–11 and 16–18; and even the sharing of the interval
E–G by such items as the C chord of measure 16, the diminished seventh

of measure 17, and the cadence chord of measure 20—all foreshadow this sudden switch into e at the end of area C. We can, finally, see the B^7 (=V^7 of e) in measure 15 as a real alternative within the harmonic ambiguity of the beginning of the B phrase.

Next, the way that the C phrase builds up to this e cadence is closely linked to the foregoing. A combination of motivic quotations and harmonic processes already experienced in the previous two phrases is used in the C phrase to work around to, of all things, a G_4^6 once again. On the downbeat of measure 26 we must surely feel, the first time we listen (and, indeed, every other time we wish to tease ourselves with the purposeful structure of the musical unfolding), that we now have at least one other opportunity to experience what has twice in succession failed to happen.

Just at this point the G_4^6 switches to the e triad in a very succinct manner. The shared interval, B–G, is so clearly exploited by the treble portion of the orchestra—we hear this interval as part of the G triad in the first part of measure 26, and then as part of the e triad throughout measure 27—that we can surely see now how e has been a potential rival to G all along. A fine touch here is the D♯ in the bass of measure 26, first heard as a chromatic passing tone from D to E but then interpreted as a scalar leading tone to E once the next measure clarifies the new triad. This D♯ creates with the constant B–G the ambiguous augmented triad that straddles the G–e division (Ex. 11-8). (The situation closely resembles one discovered in the Brahms piano piece; see page 128.)

Ex. 11-8

```
B ····· B ········ B
G ····· G ········ G
                    E
            D#
        D
      ─────────────────
       (G)          (e)
      m. 26          27
```

Finally, we note that, once again, the voice part in the C phrase consistently displays the e-minor triad, which we can now take seriously (measures 23–26; note the resemblances between the use of the e triad in the voice part of this phrase and of the previous two).

Of course, the act could not end this way: the cadence in e would render rather pointless the struggles toward G that have preceded. We know, from our initial study of the ultimate orchestral cadence, that the music returns to G over the course of the final (D) phrase. However, a curious imperfection in the e-minor cadence already foreshadows this development. As noted, the harmony in the cadence is entirely straightforward. The voice line, however, has a single unresolved pitch (Ex. 11-9). Of the first four notes here, B, G, and E are triad pitches, while

Ex. 11-9

m. 28

the F♯ is a passing tone. At the end of the line the C♯ and D♯ simply connect the first B and final E by passing tones (properly raised, according to the e-minor scale). The only pitch that does not behave so properly is the A, which may well arise from the previous downbeat G, but surely does not resolve back to G (as neighbor) or up to B (as passing tone). At the end of the phrase the A is left hanging; more important, with no more vocal music to appear in the act, the A seems rather *permanently* unresolved (at least in that timbre).[1]

To realize the full import of this tiny detail, it may be helpful to imagine some alternatives. First, picture this as the *end* of a composition (with no music to follow to pick up the A). Such a situation would leave the discordant (nontriadic) A sounding in our memory. This would not be the case if, for example, B substituted for A (Ex. 11–10). Here the B

Ex. 11-10

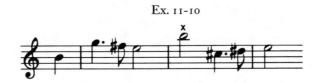

is entirely understood in its own right—so much so that we can overlook the dissonant skip it forms with the C♯ (especially since we can also

---

1. Imagine, for example, the end of a flute-piano duo in C where the flute finishes on a B and the piano, one measure later, sounds the final C chord. A disturbing sense of noncompletion would linger on after the music.

understand the function of the C♯); the B is a perfectly fine pitch to be left unsucceeded in that register, because of its triadic status.

Alternatively, imagine that the A were retained in a new version, but justified by immediate resolution to G (Ex. 11–11).

Ex. 11-11

The marring of this cadence, even in so slight a way, is understandable in terms of the inappropriateness of the key reached at this point. But the particular detail is of the greatest importance. For the question of improperly resolved A's was just our focus in the final cadence (and in the first phrase), and we can see this A as one other example. It is then picked up in measure 51, and finally, but unsatisfactorily, delivered to G in the next measure; and its reappearance in measure 53 only delays one last, flawed arrival at G, as we first observed. If we turned the page to the beginning of Act II, or listened in after intermission at the opera, we would immediately encounter the pitch-class A, still very much alive!

A few brief comments on the very difficult D phrase, which has as its function the harmonic movement from e to G, will suffice for our present purposes.

When e is established, in measure 30, it is, typically, expressed by a motive. The rising dotted-quarter–eighth arpeggio is a standard way of expressing a chord in the *Ring* (in addition to its specific dramatic significance). We note here that the next transposition of this motive is to C (measures 32–33); the shared interval is E–G, and the e triad will shortly give over its other third, G–B, to the G triad. With C as the IV and G as the I of G, the e triad gives over its materials to G, from which triad it originally borrowed its materials over the course of the A, B, and C areas.

Much of the difficult music after measure 39 derives from earlier portions of the act. But a clear orientation will be found in the establishment of a long D pedal, starting under the pinnacle G in measure 39, and lasting uninterrupted (in several octave positions) until the fundamental "V" at measure 49, resolving to G two measures later. The peak

G in measure 39 represents the highest pitch of the orchestral finish (see the G's in measures 30–32, as well as those in 47–48)—up to measure 51. At that point, and after the climb back up from D, it is cleanly knocked out of place by the high A!

A Study of Debussy:
Prelude VIII for Piano (Book I)
("La Fille aux cheveux de lin")

In this final study we confront some new features of background triad influence. The way in which this Debussy prelude projects its tonic triad differs somewhat from all other such projections we have studied, but is, on the other hand, probably fairly typical of a whole style of tonal composition. The "French impressionist" manner may be thought of as just another approach to the problem, previously introduced,[1] of the aging of the tonal system and the consequent "stretching" by composers of its properties and relations.

Clearly, the triad still underlies the music, providing meaning for each detail. But, as seen in the previous two studies, the relation between the detail and the triad may be a little more distant than in earlier, more direct tonal music.

A striking case in point is the very first formation in this prelude. For five and a half beats a solo line is forged from materials consisting of Db, Bb, Gb and Eb (Ex. 12–1). The solo nature of the presentation and the demarcating effect of the phrase-line indication separate the line from the ensuing music, suggesting its role as a generator of activity of all kinds. We have certainly encountered many items in tonal pieces that

---

1. Page 128. See also the Conclusion.

Ex. 12-1

were not themselves triads, but could be understood in terms of triads.
What is unusual and challenging here is that this nontriad is the very
first detail of a piece, and so cannot be considered in any local context
until such a context may be established.

Now if the item under consideration were a dominant seventh, then,
though it would not itself be a triad, it could instantly bring to mind the
triad to which it usually refers; thus the event would be comprehensible.
But this "minor-minor" seventh type clearly does not suggest any particular orientation; in fact (and unlike the dominant-seventh type) this
collection subsumes *two* complete, stable triads—Gb and eb (Ex. 12–2).
So no particular triad is uniquely suggested, and, to compound the initial
confusion in the piece, two triads are present.

Ex. 12-2

$$\overline{E^\flat \ldots\ldots G^\flat \ldots\ldots B^\flat \ldots\ldots D^\flat}$$

The form this tune takes seems to exploit the double-triad possibilities
of the unit that underlies it. As a very first impression, we hear the Gb
triad (first three attacked notes). This impression is weakened immediately as the Gb is not emphasized, but merely moved through. In fact,
the Eb is now the long, on-the-beat note, and, with the three sixteenth
attacks in a row that lead into the Eb, the eb triad seems emphasized. Regular groupings into three, leading to each beat, then alternate the emphasis
between the two triads. Furthermore, the tune connects Eb and Db, back
and forth; these two pitches are, at most, the difference between the Gb
and eb triads; and the shared material, Gb–Bb, forms the connecting link
between them.

While we listen to this ambiguous opening we can ponder the theoret-
ical possibilities. If the notes are to "mean" in terms of the Gb triad, then
Eb must eventually prove to be an upper-neighbor to Db (the closest
Gb triad tone) (Ex. 12–3). On the other hand, with eb as possible refer-

Ex. 12-3

$$D\flat \frown D\flat$$
$$B\flat \frown B\flat$$
$$G\flat \smile G\flat$$
$$E\flat \longrightarrow D\flat$$

ence, the Db would have to be neighbor to Eb (Ex. 12–4). But the second choice here is hardly possible; for normal linear practice in the minor scale would require a D♮, not a Db, as lower neighbor to an Eb tonic.

Ex. 12-4

$$D\flat \longrightarrow E\flat$$
$$B\flat \frown B\flat$$
$$G\flat \frown G\flat$$
$$E\flat \smile E\flat$$

If the Gb interpretation thus seems more probable, certain details of the solo opening may serve to predict a Gb resolution for this chord, in the manner of example 12–3. The initial note, Db, is much longer than any other note in the passage; it belongs exclusively to the Gb world, and thus places emphasis quite clearly in that direction. Second, as the passage draws to a close (the chord at the end of measure 2 clearly beginning a new grouping), the melody settles on Gb as final note, with the bottom third of the Gb triad clearly displayed. In one sense, this may just represent the isolating of the shared Gb–Bb interval, thus emphasizing the ambiguity; but the sense of settling on Gb must surely link up with the strong beginning on Db to provide a sense of the Gb triad through the skeletal, defining fifth that spans the triad as it spans the phrase.

In fact, a clear Gb resolution is just what takes place next, bringing with it a definitive close to an opening phrase that lasts for the first three and a half measures. What is sustained for four beats, starting at least by beat two of measure 3, is purely the Gb triad. The last attacked note of that triad is the treble Db, which comes off a treble arpeggiation of the triad interval Gb–Db, connected by passing tones. This Db must be the long-range resolution of the troubling Eb sustained throughout the solo part of the phrase in exactly that registral position (refer to example 12–3). In fact, the detail starting on the last eighth of measure 2, Gb–Eb–Gb (which balances the Gb–Bb–Gb that ends the solo line), serves to bring in the Eb in conjunction with the same Gb that moves stepwise down to the resolving Db, thus making the connection explicit (Ex. 12–5). The

Ex. 12-5

(compare with Ex. 12-3)

impressive length of the Gb chord, and particularly the length of the final Db melodic pitch (so much longer than any earlier melody note), seems to prove the point. We can now think back to our experiences in certain Brahms passages, where a neighboring pitch would receive so much emphasis that the sense in which it would be said to depend on another pitch is strained.[2] Here, clearly, we strain our triadic imagination until the end of the phrase. The length to which the situation is protracted must also be reminiscent of Wagner's technique of reference suspension.[3]

And yet the phrase is still puzzling. We have not bothered to mention the only other item in the opening measures, the Cb chord on the last eighth of measure 2, the first explicit harmonic sonority in the piece. This chord matches well the Gb–Eb melodic interval above it, since those pitches are part of the Cb triad (as well as the eb triad). At the same time, the chord introduces an Eb in the bass register, which then moves directly to Db on the next downbeat, thus summarizing the essential Eb–Db motion that is unfolding an octave above in less explicit form, and is of course the clue to the entire phrase. The problem is, Gb is here tonicized not by the usual V or V[7] means, but plagally (IV–I). Therefore Gb is not introduced with a leading tone, or even with a second degree (2–1 melodic resolution). In fact, the seventh and second scale steps are the only missing pitch classes in the otherwise complete Gb diatonic collection within the first phrase!

In this music, however, the IV seems perfectly appropriate in a way that the more usual V or V[7] could not be. For it forms one more link in the thirds-sharing chain begun in the opening solo (Ex. 12–6). Notice

2. See, for example, measure 9 of the Brahms composition.
3. See measures 9–14 of the *Walküre* excerpt, page 136.

Ex. 12-6

```
D♭                          /D♭\
B♭   B♭                     | B♭ |
G♭   G♭   G♭                | G♭ |
     E♭   E♭                | E♭ |
          C♭                \ C♭ /
─────────────────
(G♭)  (e♭)  (C♭)
```

here that the e♭ triad is entirely subsumed by the other two, with both its thirds being shared (the G♭ and C♭ chords each share only one interval with another chord in the group). So the e♭ chord, at the end of the solo line, gives over its thirds to the G♭ tonicization: G♭–B♭ to I and G♭–E♭ to IV of G♭. It is also interesting to note that G♭ is the only pitch class shared by *all three* triads, and thus emerges as tonic focus for all.

This opening phrase, with its unusual treatment of the tonic triad, conditions the behavior of tonal materials in the rest of the composition. From the overall form and styling of the piece, through the goals and formations of individual phrases, down to the formation and appropria- tion of local details, the entire prelude reflects its first phrase. We will concentrate on some features of this relation on all levels, and indicate others.

One immediate manifestation of the influence of the initial phrase is the prominence of the three triads of the phrase (G♭, C♭, e♭) as the music develops. Throughout the piece we encounter declarative in- stances of these three stations (the e♭ sometimes in major), among which we mention the following: measure 6, beat 3, the E♭ triad; measures 10–11, the G♭ chord prolonged; measures 12–13, a V–I motion in G♭, above a G♭ pedal; measure 14, the C♭ triad initiating a new configuration; measure 16, the C♭ triad; measure 19, the E♭ triad, prolonged throughout measures 20 and 21; third beat of measure 21, the C♭ triad; measure 23, the C♭ triad; measure 28, the C♭ triad; measure 31, the e♭ triad; measure 32, the G♭ triad; measure 33 (downbeat), the C♭ triad; and the final four measures, the G♭ triad sustained as cadential element.

Now among these, all of which may act as familiar signposts along the way, some are clearly projected as focal points in the overall move- ment of the piece. The very first stopping point after the first phrase, to begin with, is the E♭ triad in measure 6. This item is tonicized by its

own applied dominant, the immediately preceding Bb chord. The Bb–
Eb succession appears earlier in this second phrase, and in a form diatonic
to the Gb tonic key (measure 5). Thus a link is formed between the less
explicit appearance of eb in the opening phrase and its local establishment
at the end of the second phrase. Notice that the eb interval Eb–Gb (end of
measure 4) is the first detail to follow the cadence of the first phrase.
(Its articulative connection to the first phrase will be considered shortly.)
The only other chords present in the second phrase are Gb and Db. The
Gb, of course, is already familiar. But the Db harmony, quite prominent
in this phrase, is actually the first appearance of V in the music. Rather
than functioning as a dominant to Gb, however, the Db chords (downbeats of measures 5 and 6) seem placed in direct, and balancing, opposi-
tion to the eb/Eb chords (the only other stressed points in these two
measures), resulting in an expansion and echo of the original Db/Eb alternation in the opening solo.

The next such landmark is surely the Gb prolongation in measures 10–
11, which forms the ending of the third phrase of the piece. Over the
course of the three phrases, then, the music has progressed from Gb to Eb
and back; rather than reflecting the tonic triad, this relation must grow
out of the alternations of the Gb and eb triads in the first solo formation.
In this middle-range level, then, we can already see the influence of the
peculiarities of the first-presented Gb world at work.

The establishment of Cb, the subdominant region, in measure 16 (the
next comparable phrase demarcation) seems to expand upon the original
plagal establishment of Gb in the opening phrase: the Gb chords of measures 10–13 have given way to the locally stable Cb cadential chord in
measure 16. It is particularly interesting to note that here Cb is tonicized
by way of *its* subdominant chord, the Fb triad struck on the downbeat
of, and prolonged throughout, measure 15. Thus the connection to the
original use of the Cb chord, in measure 2, is made explicit; and we see
that the behavior of chords in the earliest measures conditions their behavior here.

The music next takes a turn into Eb, starting with the downbeat of
measure 19. This tonality is experienced as a direct substitute for Gb,
for the tonicized Cb in measure 16 seemed to be about to return to the Gb
from which it arose: in measure 17 an Ab⁷ chord acts as V of V for Gb
(moving directly to Db⁷ on the second beat); instead of the V⁷ now

moving to a tonic Gb, the formula begins to repeat in measure 18, with
the reappearance of the V/V; this time, however, the Ab chord resolves
deceptively—to Bb (a V–vi motion, basically), which now acts as dominant to Eb. With the establishment of Eb by way of applied V–I motion
now, the diatonic collection of Eb, within a clear Eb-triad frame, persists
until the end of measure 21. This long-range substitution of Eb for Gb is
a direct outgrowth of the activity in the opening phrase.

The ultimate reestablishment of Gb comes about gradually, and is
certainly expected to be associated with the recapitulation of the opening
line that comes in measure 28. But just at that point Cb substitutes for Gb,
again foiling a V/V–V set-up in the previous measure. Above this sustained IV chord the opening melody, with its Gb/eb combination, is
sounded; the result is, of course, all three basic triads simultaneously.
Before IV moves into I (which it did succinctly at the end of the first
phrase), a prominent eb statement is interposed (measure 31). The succession of downbeats in measures 28 (=29=30), 31, and 32 thus defines
the three essential formations. In this recapitulation, then, the three
germinal chords appear both simultaneously and in succession. Significantly, Gb is the last in this series, as it is, next, the final formation in the
composition, exclusively occupying the last four measures.

Over the course of the piece we have seen, then, that not only does a
succession of prominent items reflect the construction of the initial
phrase, but also the overall harmonic process, by phrases, plays out the
possibilities inherent in the generating complex. We turn now to various
interesting local details, which will reveal the pervasive influence of this
generator on other levels.

Inherent in the original four-note figure is another shape, derivable
by extending into neighboring registers the original notes (Ex. 12–7).

Ex. 12-7

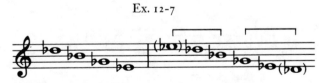

That is, the Eb and Db step relation is originally only present as a seventh.
Potentially, however, the actual step can arise, and, because of the sym-
metry of the four-note complex (a major third with minor thirds on

Ex. 12-8

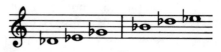

each side), this step will in both directions be associated with an adjacent minor third (Ex. 12–8). This figure becomes a major motivic shape in the music, and makes its first appearance at a transposition consisting entirely of "original" pitches, growing directly out of the first phrase cadence (measure 4). The melody descends into Db in the cadence, only to turn around back to Eb (the Db–Eb alternation reduced now to step range). Moving then to Gb, the melody has retraced its steps from the cadence point (downbeat of measure 3). In so doing, the major-second–minor-third figure is first produced. We should notice that the form of the cadence, with Eb originally resolving to Db, already makes use of this shape (Ex. 12–9).

This step-skip shape is used to generate the melody of measure 12 (Ex. 12–10). The tail of this melody, also, is familiar as the scalar con-

Ex. 12-9

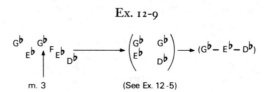

clusion to the opening phrase, heard again in more extended fashion in the repetition of the opening cadence that occurs in measures 10–11.

Ex. 12-10

The three-note figure can be seen again in measures 15 and 17–18, and, because of our experience (Ex. 12–9) in hearing the embedded version of the figure in the opening cadence, we can also identify its appearance in the Eb cadence of measure 19 (Ex. 12–11). The Eb music

Ex. 12-11

that follows is thoroughly pervaded by this figure, as is, in less obvious form, the modulatory music that begins thereafter (Ex. 12–12). Finally, this configuration makes its last appearance in the rising sixteenths in measure 35.

Ex. 12-12

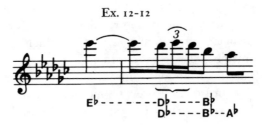

Another strand of detail emanating from the opening phrase is vertical rather than linear. Pure triads are the only vertical forms sounded in the first phrase, but the four-note melodic figure of the opening soon serves as a model for vertical sonority. This is a likely development, in terms of the initial harmonic ambiguity: in the first moments of the solo we hear neither the G♭ nor the e♭ triads in isolation, but a nontriadic combination of the two instead (which includes, thus, the "step" relation as a harmonic interval). Through the second phrase we still hear only pure triads; but in phrase three we suddenly meet dominant-seventh types (beginning with the downbeat of measure 8) that do not act like dominant sevenths. Clearly, these sonorities are not meant *as* dominant sevenths, but are imitations of the opening sonority. Of course, the two intervallic collections (the dominant-seventh type and the "minor-minor-seventh" type) are not *equivalent;* but the generalization "triad with step (seventh) added" subsumes both formations. In particular, note that both omit the half-step (major-seventh) sound, the inclusion of which in any such chord might immediately signal a contrast. (Such a development takes place further on in the piece.)

The series of seventh chords in measures 8–9 consists of chords a whole step apart, in alternation. Thus, the alternation of the original D♭

and Eb is invoked; in fact, Db and Eb—members, respectively, of the two alternated chords here—are specifically alternated (in the alto voice).

The next sonority, on beat three of measure 9, is exactly our original minor-minor-seventh type: in fact, it is precisely the four notes of the opening solo. Thus a standard for vertical sound emerges at this point.

Even the V–I motions that begin appearing now (the first such normal confirmations of the tonic) reflect this sonority notion. In the third phrase, measure 9, the cadence melody, Gb–Eb–Gb (as in the original phrase, just repeated here), is now accompanied by the chords V^7–I (as opposed to the original plagal cadence). The V^7 is thus matched with the melodic Gb, producing a complex that consists of the usual triadic intervals plus the added step relation (in the form of a seventh) due to the presence of the "anticipatory" Gb (which in the original was just a normal member of the IV chord).

The expanded V–I motion in measures 12–13 works the same way. The downbeat chord of measure 12 appears as a combination of I and V (with I below, as a pedal, and V rolled above); Eb, the melodic pitch, is added to this complex, and the result is once again a mixture of triadic intervals plus major seconds.

The added Eb on the downbeat of measure 12 is of course a pitch affixed to the previous two melodic pitches (which are safely within the Gb triad of the previous measure) to form the minor-third–major-second figure discussed above, and leading into the figure-generated passage shown in example 12–10. Harmonically this line matches the V–I resolution pattern in that all of its notes either are Gb-triad notes themselves, or (on the model of the original first-phrase cadence) resolve by step into Gb-triad notes in the next measure. The most delayed of these resolutions is the Eb attacked on the last beat, which moves to the Db in measure 13 much the same way that Eb moves to Db in measures 2–3. These resolutions demonstrate the underlying grammatical similarity between such "new" expressions and the more usual relations we have studied (Ex. 12–13). A point of repose, on beat two of measure 13, represents the completion of all resolution.

The sonority notions we have been discussing take a new turn in the next passages, beginning in measure 14. Here all voices move up and down by thirds (with scalar passing tones). One result, pictured in Ex. 12–14, is the extension of the triad-subsuming chain of thirds (see

Ex. 12-13

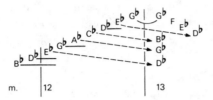

Ex. 12–2 and then Ex. 12–6) to include the Fb chord on the downbeat of measure 15, which acts as the IV of Cb for the Cb cadence in the next measure. The passage begins with the Cb triad (just the *lowest* item on the chain established in the first phrase, but now the highest in this "continuation"), passes through the ab triad (the next triad in the chain) on

Ex. 12-14

beat three of measure 14 (the melody is delayed, but reaches the pitch Eb during the beat, to form the pure chord), and arrives at the Fb chord on the next downbeat.[4]

A second result, however, is due to the staggering of the voices (the delays in the melody) and the initial move up a third in the melody. This is the revelation of the *half-step* relation in this thirds chain; for as we moved down the thirds chain one step below the Gb triad (in the opening passage), a major second was produced (the seventh between Db and Eb), which then became a normal part of vertical sonorities; and now,

4. If the triads in the chain of thirds of Ex. 12–14 are numbered 1 through 5 from top to bottom, then these items develop as follows: 1 and 2 form the opening solo sonority (measures 1–2); 3 is the first vertical chord (end of measure 2); 3 is then resumed on the downbeat of measure 14 and repeated on the next beat (again allowing for the delay in the melody line); 4 occurs on beat three, and 5 emerges on the next downbeat. But, in fact, the entire chain can be seen to develop at once if we begin with the Gb chord of measure 13 and connect it to the Cb chord of measure 14 by way of the intermediary eb chord formed there by the initial motion of the melody with the downbeat Eb!

moving further, the *major* seventh (half-step type) is included[5] (as between Bb and Cb in beat one of measure 14), and now forms a part of many sonorities. This half-step sound is a vertical feature of the entire measure, but can soon be seen in such chords as the downbeats of measures 17 and 18. Thereafter the sonority repertory is permanently expanded.[6]

The climax in use of these sonorities comes in the (ironically) soft passage (the first pianissimo!) beginning in measure 24. Here the first eight chords are all built out of the first four notes of the piece (thus all lines as well as chords are so structured); and the two quarter-note triad mixtures represent the triad + whole step and triad + half step outgrowths of the first four-note model. Meanwhile, the entire passage is grounded in normal tonal meaning, with the first eight chords prolonging a I triad, and the two one-beat chords presenting essentially IV and V; the passage continues to the deceptive cadence on the downbeat of measure 28 (previously described).

The end of the piece is true to its beginning. The actual cadence into the tonic chord of measure 36 is nondominant, and, in fact, clearly invokes the plagal cadence of the first phrase: the last notes of measure 35, those that actually move directly into the tonic chord, are the Cb and Eb of the IV chord. And once that terminal tonic is reached, no V–I confirmation follows. Rather, what would be the roots of the dominant and tonic triads, Db and Gb respectively, are struck in succession; both pitches, however, are members of the tonic triad, which is sustained meanwhile.

It can safely be said, in fact, that not a single genuine, unspoiled dominant–tonic motion occurs anywhere in the piece; it should be noted that the V[7] at the end of measure 23 resolves not to a pure Gb chord, but to the Gb-expressing four-note complex; that the V chord at the end of measure 27 resolves deceptively; and that the V chords of the V–I motions in measures 9–10 and 12–13 are spoiled by the addition of antici-

---

5. This is due to the diatonic restriction placed on the expansion down by thirds. This diatonic rule is broken to introduce Eb, to provide a genuine applied IV for the Cb cadence. But notice the repeat of this phrase starting in measure 33, which is strictly diatonic.

6. From triads to triads + whole step to triads + half step, the harmonic vocabulary has expanded in two stages, represented by the two thirds-chain passages of measures 1–2 and 14. These two passages are further linked, however, in that the second one seems to be an augmentation of the first; the direct motion by thirds in measure 1 has become gradual motion by thirds (in all voices, now moving together in augmentation of the original single voice) filled in with passing tones.

patory or pedal tones. The V chord, we might note, can be developed by climbing in thirds from the root of the tonic triad in the upward direction (Gb–Bb–Db–F–Ab, diatonically within the tonic collection), while the subdominant is won in the opposite manner (see examples 12–6 and 12–14). As set forth in the opening passage, this music seems to be concerned with a mirror-image world discovered *underneath* the triad. This is music of the tonal system viewed somewhat upside down.

Conclusion

About the nature, meaning, intent, and spirit of musical analysis, much was left unsaid in the introduction to these studies, and little or nothing was added after the first chapter. Such an omission was not meant to foreshadow a lengthy postmortem here reflecting on what analysis means in terms of what we have just accomplished. Rather it was a purposeful evasion, in the hopes that from all the foregoing much could be inferred about at least one style of analysis. Indeed such matters ought to be confronted directly, but perhaps not here. The purpose of this concluding word is not to look back, but to look ahead.

It is obvious that a gross restriction has governed the selection of compositions studied here, which have included only pieces written *after* the tonal system seemed by common practice to be fully formed, and *before* that system was left aside by the general compositional community. Automatically, then, the triad became the fundamental tool, concept, and resource in these pages.

Thus, from the foregoing experiences, incorrect inferences about the intersecting and overlapping meanings of "the triad," "musical compositions," "musical meaning," and "analysis" might too easily be drawn. Of course in the very first chapter the triad was in a sense *developed* as an interpretative tool, and then posited as a general and pervasive referential element. Thereafter the place of the triad in our work was, although constantly demonstrated, simply assumed. The point is, this assumption was a direct product of the nature of the restriction placed on the pieces chosen.

Now if similar analytic techniques were applied to a composition by, for example, Arnold Schoenberg, we would find that only a portion—just the "pretriadic" portion, or that consisting of observations made on the surface character of a passage and not depending on specific pitch grammar—of these techniques would work. And by "work" we mean that a piece so studied should eventually appear rationally constructed, at least in the sense that a listener could objectively communicate to someone a perceived coherence in the piece. For such nontonal pieces surely behave as *pieces*, though not as *tonal* pieces. That is, some other mode of coherence, not having anything to do with the triad, may be operative, and might be discoverable. Since no truly common practice has emerged since the tonal one, often this coherence must be discovered anew, for each piece, at disturbingly deep levels.

The problem is more extensive than it may first appear. Consider, for example, the following passage from a piano piece by Schoenberg (Opus 23, No. 1) (Ex. 13–1). If we try to understand the pitches of this passage

Ex. 13–1

From *Fünf Klavierstücke* by Arnold Schoenberg, Edition Wilhelm Hansen. Reprinted by permission of the publisher.

in terms of some triadic background[1] the piece will undoubtedly appear incoherent, random, or just badly composed. But if, on the other hand, we proceed to notice that the first and last chords in the passage, though not triads, are yet three-note repositories of intervallic information that is useful in interpreting the lines, the passage may begin to take on some meaning for us. Just as we describe a triad sonority as one resulting from the mixture of the intervallic qualities of the major third, the minor third and the perfect fifth, we can describe these polar chords as, respectively, a minor second + major second + minor third; and a minor second + minor third + major third (spelling notwithstanding). These intervals

---

1. In the sense that, as we have seen in our Brahms, Wagner, and Debussy studies, nontriadic-looking configurations can, if found in a plainly *triadic context*, ultimately be understood triadically. As this was more difficult with later tonal music, it may be impossible here. Hence we do not think of the music as tonal.

are the only ones found in the lines emanating from the first chord and arriving in the second. And, in fact, all along the way we can pick out trichords of adjacent notes that form one or the other intervallic collection precisely (Ex. 13–2).

Ex. 13-2

It might be imagined, then, that all we need do is posit some referential intervallic representative that can generate many objects found in some music we are dealing with. Once we have found this referential "key," perhaps the nontonal piece will begin to read out as plainly as will, say, a French sentence once we have discarded our English dictionary and begun to use a French one to interpret the sounds we encounter. If we can at least believe in the plausibility of such an approach, perhaps some of the implicit prejudice most listeners bring to the hearing of nontonal music will be dispelled.

But a little reflection on the complexity of the tonal system, as we have witnessed it in these studies, will suggest that such a notion can hardly be sufficient, even in a most rudimentary sense. For in tonal music we certainly don't expect all surface formations to *be* triads; certainly, most tunes are not, in themselves, triads. Rather, we begin to discover that all things in tonal pieces *relate to* triads by way of some kind of grammar that mediates between the triad as a concept and the piece as a reality.

So, having avoided the pitfall of insisting that to be "music" a sound succession must involve the triad, we do not wish to fall into the trap of being satisfied with the mere relatability of a list of atonal objects. Rather, we should like to settle for nothing less than a grammar, every bit as rich and productive as the tonal one, for our nontonal music.

But if there is some music that moves us (though not according to the triad), perhaps just the realization that we *might* develop some grammatical tools can inspire us to imagine that the music could be analyzed. Such analysis, then, would indicate that we were learning to experience the music in a comprehensible, detailed way; and in so justifying our response to the music, we would be approaching it with the same respect we have paid to the tonal pieces whose "insides" and "outsides" we have been learning to relate.

In any case, one can begin by falling back on some general ways of perceiving and slicing musical surfaces developed earlier. One will then be hearing post-tonal music already, at some primitive level, *in the same way* that one begins hearing tonal music. Whatever divergences may then take place at more complex levels of understanding, at least a common juncture will have been found, enabling us to include both tonal and nontonal "types" under a unified notion of "music"—and a destructive and limiting prejudice may be on its way to dissolution. Such an attitude would be its own reward: the richness that may unfold, in the presence of the finest post-tonal music, would speak eloquently for itself.